THE MINISTRY OF THE WORD

THE MINISTRY OF THE WORD

WILLIAM M. TAYLOR

BAKER BOOK HOUSE
Grand Rapids, Michigan

Reprinted 1975 by
Baker Book House
ISBN: 0-8010-8830-5

PHOTOLITHOPRINTED BY CUSHING - MALLOY, INC.
ANN ARBOR, MICHIGAN, UNITED STATES OF AMERICA
1975

Introduction

William Mackergo Taylor (1829-1895)
The Ministry of the Word

Scottish-born, graduate of Glasgow University and Edinburgh United Presbyterian Divinity Hall, Taylor was pastor of Presbyterian churches at Kilmauris, Scotland, and Liverpool, England. He transferred to the Congregational body when he was called to the Broadway Tabernacle, New York City (1872-1892). His vital preaching was recognized early when he was invited, in 1876, to be the third of the Lyman Beecher Lecturers. He was invited to be the lecturer again in 1886. Only a few men have appeared twice in that lecture series.

Taylor's evangelical spirit, sound learning, constant devotion to study and running style, combined to evoke wide responses to his messages, both from those who sat under him and those who read his published works which still endure. The reissue of this volume is indicative of a value beyond the ordinary. Principles and guidelines for the student and preacher are shared in vivid and arresting style.

We learn about the nature of the ministry and its grand design, the preacher's preparation, and the demands made on a minister who maintains high ideals. Expository preaching is stressed and the doctrines of our faith are taught with insight gained from much Bible study and a burning conviction to preach the word. His intimate knowledge of people prevents abstract notions and theoretic ideas from crowding out true pastoral preaching. His sermons ring with Christian realism.

This book is especially timely in that Taylor emphatically counsels to write, write, write! From this preparation in his study, the preacher becomes aware of the excellence demanded by pastoral preaching: a fertile mind, acquaintance with the best in literature, devotion to Biblical meditation and sermon construction. *The Ministry of the Word* may well encourage today's preacher to emulate Taylor's dedication, for it is the ministry of the *word* which abides and is life-giving.

RALPH G. TURNBULL

PREFACE.

THIS book is not a Treatise on Homiletics. Neither is it a ministerial autobiography. But it is an attempt to give to my younger brethren in the pulpit, and to those who are preparing for the ministry, some practical hints which I should have been thankful to have received twenty years ago, and which have been suggested to me as much by the blunders as by the successes of my public life.

To my seniors they may seem to be of little importance; but I was not writing for them. My aim has been to set before my readers a few first principles emphasized by experience; and if my book shall be to any young minister like the hand of an elder brother held back to help him forward, I shall rejoice even more than he.

The course was prepared especially for the theological students of Yale College, as the " Lyman Beecher Lectures" for 1876; but selections from it were delivered also to the members of Union, Princeton, and Oberlin Theological Seminaries.

To these young brethren with whom I have been brought so pleasantly into fellowship, to the members of the Faculties of the Seminaries which I have named, and to all interested in the education of " the Sons of the Prophets," I dedicate this volume, with the prayer that He " whose I am, and whom I serve," may make it largely useful to those who are preparing to give themselves to " the ministry of the Word."

New York, *April* 1876.

CONTENTS.

LECTURE I.

THE NATURE AND DESIGN OF THE CHRISTIAN MINISTRY.

LECTURE I.

THE NATURE AND DESIGN OF THE CHRISTIAN MINISTRY.

" WHAT can the man do that cometh after the King?" My two distinguished predecessors in this Lectureship, unmindful of the generous order of Boaz to his reapers, to "let fall some of the handfuls of purpose" for the poor Gentile gleaner, have so thoroughly swept the field, that nothing is left for me save here and there an ear. This would be hard for anyone; how much more for one who has to confess that he is, as yet, a learner in the department in which they are masters! For two and twenty years I have been striving to reach my ideal of the Christian preacher, and it seems to me as if I were to-day as far from it as ever. Always as I have appeared to advance towards it, it has fled before me, and still it hovers above and beyond me, beckoning me on to some attainment yet unrealized. Never did it seem to me so difficult to preach as it does to-day. The magnitude of the work grows upon me the longer I engage in it; and with every new

attempt I make, there comes the painful consciousness that I have not yet attained. Twenty years ago,
I thought I could preach a little, and flattered myself that I knew something about Homiletics. Now
I feel that I am but a beginner, and the thought of
addressing you upon such a subject fills me with dis-
may. Still we may get on well together, if only you
will consent to regard me as a fellow-student, or
at least as an elder brother, striving with you after
the same end, and speaking to you out of the fullness of his heart, that he may warn you to avoid the
mistakes which he has made, and stimulate you to
aim after that efficiency on which his own heart is
set.

The nature of this Lectureship requires that he
who holds it, for the time, should deal with the subject, as illustrated by his own experience. It may
be well, therefore, in the outset, that I should mention one or two cautions which need to be kept in
mind by you, while we are proceeding with our addresses.

In the first place, it must be fully understood by
you, that no one can begin precisely at that point at
which another has arrived only after long years of
persevering effort. The son of the merchant entering
upon the possession of his father's fortune, may commence housekeeping on the same scale as his parents.
But, even then, it has been generally seen that he is
deficient in those qualities of character which were
most distinctive in his father, and which in him were
formed by the struggle through which he wrestled up

to his success. You may acquire a legacy in a moment, but you cannot, all at once, step into that homiletic habit which it has taken another long years to form, and by which he is able at a glance to see into the heart of a subject, and to know precisely how to treat it so as to impress his hearers most deeply with its importance. You cannot obtain, as one might say, ready-made, that ease in work and fluency in utterance which it has taken him almost a lifetime to acquire.

Some, indeed, have, from the very first, manifested such skill in handling subjects, and such eloquence in discoursing on them, that we may fairly speak of them as men of genius, in this peculiar department. But these are the exceptions. The great majority of those who have become eminent in the pulpit, have grown into their greatness. They have, under God, made themselves for their position, by watchful self-discipline, and steady perseverance. Now, you cannot reach the end at which they have arrived, without using means similar to those which they employed. At first they were, as you are now, inexperienced, and, perhaps, also somewhat censorious, more skillful in criticising the sermons of others than in sermonizing for themselves. But at length, inspired by love to Christ and to the souls of men, they have been led so to train themselves for their work, that they have become truly great.

Behind the present ability of such men as these, there is a history which must never be lost sight of, for if without their history you try to perform their work,

in their particular way, you will inevitably and ignominiously fail.   Thus, one tells us that he prepares his
sermons on the Lord's day on which they are delivered;
and that he never writes more than the merest outline
of them ; and you know that thousands hang with
breathless interest upon his lips.   But that is the
ultimatum at which he has arrived, after a lifetime of
such experiences as have rarely fallen to the lot of
any man, and after a discipline which has been in
some respects as thorough as it has been peculiar.
Now, if you begin by trying to do as he is doing now,
you will be as successful mistakes as David would have
been in the armor of Saul.

Another describes to us how he has discarded the use,
if not also the preparation, of a manuscript, and as you
listen to his stately eloquence, and see the magnificent
ease with which he appears to sway his audiences, you
may be led to attempt, at one leap, to vault up to the
height on which he stands.   But he had to go up, by a
long series of single steps, the ascent of which involved
the labor of a quarter of a century, and what is your
puny jump to that ?

Let it be distinctly understood, then, that the value
of all such autobiographic glimpses as these friends
have given us, and as we may give, consists in the
unfolding of processes of self-culture, and in the stimulus which these impart, rather than in the commending of the particular methods which in individual
cases have been adopted.

Again, it must not be forgotten that no one man can
merge his individuality into that of another. If one is to

do anything effectively in the pulpit, or elsewhere, he must be *himself*. It is the glory of the Gospel of Christ that it lifts into itself, and transmutes into elements of power, the very personal idiosyncracies of its preachers. No one of the apostles was cast precisely in the mold of another. John, and Peter, and Paul had their distinctive features, each of which was made instrumental in bringing out some new phase of the truth which they all alike proclaimed. And as it was with them, so it is still. No preacher should try to form himself after the model of another. If you make such an attempt, you may depend upon it that what is character in your exemplar, will in you degenerate into caricature. There is something noble in a voice, but however excellent an echo may be *as an echo*, there is a hollowness and an indistinctness about it which gives it unreality. The poorest wild flower that blooms beneath the hedge, is better than the richest waxen imitation of the camelia or the rose, for it has a beauty and a fragrance of its own.

Artificiality is repulsive anywhere, but in the pulpit it is worse than offensive ; for there it robs the man of that distinctive and individual power which God has given to him for the very purpose of ministering to his efficiency. The preaching of the gospel has been committed to men, that through their very manhood it may tell the better on those whom they address ; and as each has his own particular characteristics, it will be found that in so far forth as he gives them play, he will have a power over his audience which no other man can wield. Those who have risen to the highest useful-

ness have done so through the consecration of themselves to their work. They have laid themselves—
not the poor imitations of other men—upon the altar,
and the lesson of their history is, not that we should
try to make ourselves into them, but that we should,
like them, use all our powers and develop all our individuality in the noble work in which we are engaged.

Once more: we must bear in mind, that in the ministry, as in other pursuits, success results only from
continuous and systematic labor. Usefulness is not
a mere accident. Even of Paul and Barnabas it is
recorded on one occasion that they " so spake that a
great multitude of the Jews, and also of the Greeks
believed,"* implying that there was in their discourses
a special fitness to produce conviction in the minds
of their hearers. Now, the attainment of this adaptation in our sermons requires study. It does not
come of itself. It is not in us as it was in them, the
result of a supernatural inspiration. It is the fruit of
work. True, there are some men so organized that
no amount of painstaking on their part will ever
make them effective speakers. True, again, there are
others who are by nature more highly gifted than
their fellows in the attributes of the orator; yet
even in their case the larger part of genius is perseverance; and to him who desires to succeed in persuading men by his public utterances, it must still be
said "in the sweat of thy brow shalt thou eat" this
bread also.

---

* Acts xiv. 1.

There will be many difficulties to overcome, and many excellences to be acquired. Oftentimes humiliating failures will be made; and not seldom he will be tempted to give up the whole work in utter hopelessness. But if he will only labor on, with an entire devotion to his calling, an overmastering love to his fellow-men, and a sincere desire to glorify his Lord, then he may look for some fair measure of usefulness, and may even attain to that ease and affluence of speech which, in others, he has so often contemplated with the envy of despair. When one reads of the confusion of face which attended the first efforts of such a man as Robert Hall, or of the ridiculous appearances which some of our greatest political orators have made in the outset of their careers, he will be encouraged to take heart again; for though we are not all endowed as Hall was originally, yet we may all endow ourselves with perseverance, and in the end that will tell in bringing out the best of which we are capable.

Let it never be forgotten, then, that he who would rise to eminence and usefulness in the pulpit, and become "wise in winning souls," must say of the work of the ministry, "This one thing I do." He must focus his whole heart and life upon the pulpit. He must give his days and his nights to the production of those addresses by which he seeks to convince the judgments, and move the hearts, and elevate the lives of his hearers.

All this, I know, is opposed to the common view. In the opinion of multitudes, the life of a minister is

one of ease and leisure. They see him only in the
pulpit; and as they mark the apparent "abandon" of
his manner, and listen to the easy cadence of his
speech, they think that it has cost him little. So as you
look upon the accomplished gymnast flourishing his
Indian clubs to the time of the musician, he seems to
be making little effort, and you imagine you could do
as well yourself. But try it, and you will discover
that he has acquired that graceful ease only by long
and laborious training, and that, for all so simple as
it appears to be, he is straining every muscle to its utmost, and the whole man is putting forth his energy.
Similarly in preaching, that which seems so easy, has
been made so only by strenuous exertion.

If, therefore, young gentlemen, you have chosen the
ministry, expecting to be carried to heaven " on flowery
beds of ease," you have made an egregious mistake.
With such ideas, you will never rise above the merest
drones, and you had better at once seek out some
other pursuit. But if with something like worthy
views of the design and reward of the gospel ministry you give yourselves unreservedly and wisely
to its prosecution; then, in spite of its arduous toils,
you may look for joys, the like of which this world
gives to no other laborers. "All other pleasures are
not worth its pains," and as you hear the cry of the
inquirer, "What must I do to be saved?" or the song
of the convert whom you have brought to Jesus,
there will be to you "an over-payment of delight"
for all the exertions which you have made. Through
many bitter mortifications you may have to pass:

and not seldom you may be driven to your closet, with the wailing cry of the old prophet, "Who hath believed our report?" But your very mistakes, wisely interpreted, will guide you to success; and that longing for results which yearns in your hearts will stir you up to "be strong and play the men" for Jesus and His truth.

Understand, then, that in the lectures which I am now to deliver, I do not bring to you any "short and easy method" to ministerial usefulness and success. I have nothing but the good old message of "work." You are not here, like so many tanks, to be filled up by the professors, and from which week after week the prescribed quantity is to be drawn for the supply of the people. But you are here to put on those habits of study which, though they may sit more easily on you as the years revolve, you must keep on you to the very end of your course, if at least you would be "workmen needing not to be ashamed, rightly dividing the word of truth."* But that is no hardship. That will be your very life, for it will keep you from the rust and must of decay, while at the same time it will minister to your highest happiness, provided only your hearts be in your work: for "the labor we delight in physics pain." I give you joy, therefore, in the prospect that is before you, and as one never labors so effectively as when he sings at his toil—take this as your life song:

> "I must work, through months of toil
> And years of cultivation,

---

* 2 Tim. ii. 15.

> Upon my proper patch of soil
>   To grow my own plantation.
> I'll take the showers as they fall ;
>   I will not vex my bosom ;
> Enough, if at the end of all
>   A little garden blossom."*

And now these preliminaries understood, let us advance to the consideration of our theme. I begin with the question, What is the nature and design of the Christian ministry? and for an answer to that, I open the New Testament, where I learn, in the first place, that it is especially and pre-eminently a *service.* The first minister is the Lord Jesus Christ himself; and these are His words, "Whosoever will be great among you, let him be your minister; and whosoever will be chief among you, let him be your servant; even as the son of man came not to be ministered unto, but to minister, and to give his life a ransom for many."† To the same effect are these words at the supper-table: "He that is greatest among you, let him be as the younger; and he that is chief, as he that doth serve. For whether is greater, he that sitteth at meat, or he that serveth? is not he that sitteth at meat? but I am among you as he that serveth."‡ And in harmony with the principles thus enunciated, we find that when the sons of Zebedee sought the highest places in his kingdom, he said, "Can ye drink of the cup that I drink of, and be baptized with the baptism that I am baptized with?"

---

* Tennyson's Amphion.   † Matthew xx. 26–28.
‡ Luke xxii. 26–27.

Now it is readily conceded that in these passages there are some things which are distinctive of Christ and in which we cannot perfectly resemble Him. Thus it is true that we cannot, in precisely the same sense as He did, give our lives as ransoms for many. Yet, it is none the less true, that this spirit of self-sacrifice lay at the foundation of the excellence of Christ's ministry as a whole, and gave their attractiveness to His discourses, as well as its redemptive character to His death. If, therefore, we may point to Christ's parables as models for illustration in the matter of our sermons, we may surely speak of the imitation of this consecration of Himself to the service of others, as the great indispensable prerequisite to eminence in the ministry. In doing this, indeed, we are only enforcing His own words to James and John, and urging that the drinking of Christ's cup and the submitting of ourselves to His baptism, are the only passports to real greatness in the work to which we have devoted ourselves.

This principle is far-reaching. It tells us that it is through manifold experiences of sorrow and pain that Christ fits His ministers for their highest service. He writes their best sermons for them on their own hearts with the sharp "*stylus*" of trial, and they are then most eloquent and effective when they read these off to their hearers. Those whom He calls to His ministry, He takes with Him into Gethsemane, and such as He would make the most eminent He takes the farthest in. How deeply true that is, the biographies of the most eminent preachers will amply attest!

But that is not precisely the point which I wish at this time to make out of His words. I want you to mark that this willinghood to sacrifice self in the service of others is the distinctive feature of ministerial greatness.* The people are not for the minister, but the minister is for the people; and he is to lose himself in their service and for their benefit. See how Paul had learned this lesson, when he says, "We preach not ourselves, but Christ Jesus, the Lord," *i. e.*, supplying the ellipsis "we preach not ourselves lords, but Christ Jesus, Lord, and ourselves your servants, for Jesus' sake." †

---

* It may seem to some that this is to make the Christian ministry only a higher form of ordinary discipleship. But is it, after all, in the light of the New Testament, any more than that? Unless we are prepared to accept the doctrine of "orders" with all which that involves, we must come to the view which I have here expressed. I had written the above lecture before I saw the late Principal Fairbairn's posthumous book on "Pastoral Theology," and therefore it was with great gratification that I read these sentences. "It is a fundamental principle of Christianity, that there is nothing absolutely peculiar to any one who has a place in the true Church. . . . . . If every sincere Christian can say, 'I am one with Christ, and have a personal interest in all that is His,' there can manifestly be no essential difference between Him and other believers; and whatever may distinguish any one in particular, either as regards the call to work or the capacity to work in the Lord's service, it must in kind belong to the whole community of the faithful, or else form but a subordinate characteristic. The ministry itself in its distinctive prerogatives and functions is but the more special embodiment and exhibition of those which pertain inherently to the Church, as Christ's spiritual body." (p. 64.)

† 2 Corinthians iv. 5.

Nor was this a mere momentary outflashing of sentiment with the apostle, for we find him describing it as the principle of his life that he made himself servant unto all that he might gain the more; * and even when he was explaining what seemed to his readers to be a dereliction of duty towards them, he said, " Not for that we have dominion over your faith, but are helpers of your joy." † So also Peter in exhorting the elders is careful to warn them to exercise their oversight, " not as being lords over God's heritage, but being ensamples to the flock."‡

Now I put this in the forefront, because, as it seems to me, misunderstanding here, goes very far to account for the ministerial failures over which the churches mourn, and for the partial character of the successes which have been made by many who were otherwise admirably adapted for the work. I can never forget the impression made on me in the early portion of my Liverpool ministry, when a brother who had just come with me from the study of a neighbor, where we had heard him railing for a long time against his people, said to me, " The truth is, he seems to think that the congregation exists for him, but the right-hearted minister recognizes that he exists for the congregation. Depend upon it, his work will be a failure." And a failure it was. But all unconsciously to himself, the brother who predicted that, preached a most powerful sermon to me, for if I have been blessed with the

---

* 1 Corinthians ix. 19.   † 2 Corinthians i. 24.

‡ 1 Peter v. 3.

utmost harmony between my people and myself, and if, in any measure, I have been useful to them, it has been because I have tried to remember and lay to heart these simple words.

The office of the preacher is that of a helper of his fellows. His special duty is to lead them to Him who is their Helper and Redeemer, and to assist them in the understanding of His word, and in the application of its principles to their daily lives. He is not in the ministry, in order that he may be fêted and flattered, and made the altar on which the adulation and incense of his people are to be laid. He is not set to receive the sacrifices offered by his hearers, but rather ought he to make himself a sacrifice on their behalf, aye, even though sometimes his devotion to them may be met with ingratitude ; yet, none the less is it to be continued by him. Hardly can we find a more sublime spectacle in itself, or a more appropriate model for the Christian minister, than that presented by Paul, when he says, "I will very gladly spend and be spent for you ; though the more abundantly I love you, the less I be loved." *

And yet, all this abnegation of self is perfectly consistent with a proper magnifying of the ministerial office, and is, though it may seem paradoxical to say it, the surest means of obtaining the affection and honor of the people. He who is always hungering for these things, and watching whether or not they will be rendered to him, never

---

* 2 Corinthians xii. 15.

gets them; while he who seeks to be the servant of all—comforting the sorrowful, assisting the weak, sustaining the burdened, directing the perplexed, and cheering the disconsolate—will, as he is pursuing his work, gather round him the love and confidence of his people, so that in time of trial they shall be a living wall of defence around him against all his adversaries. Whosoever will be great in this field, therefore, must begin by renouncing self. If you make yourself the end of your ambition, you will lose your labor, and do no good either to yourself or to others; but if forgetting self, you seek the good of your fellows for Christ's sake, you will bless them, and have at last their happiness added to your own. In all matters of meanness, or duplicity, or corruption, stand upon your dignity, and do not let yourselves stoop to perform them; but in all matters of loving service, seek your dignity through their performance, for usefulness and eminence, like wisdom, are "ofttimes nearer when we stoop, than when we soar." Thus, the motto of the ministry is that of the highest nobility, "Ich Dien," I SERVE; and he who most worthily acts out its meaning is already in one of its loftiest places.

But to complete our idea of the nature of the ministry, we must take into consideration the end which in his life of service the preacher is to keep in view. Now, we find that, also, clearly set before us in the New Testament, for Paul, in tracing up the origin of the ministry to the gift of the ascended

Christ, has said, " He gave some, apostles ; and some, prophets ; and some, evangelists ; and some, pastors and teachers ; for the perfecting of the saints ; for the work of the ministry ; for the edifying of the body of Christ : till we all come in the unity of the faith, and of the knowledge of the Son of God, unto a perfect man, unto the measure of the stature of the fulness of Christ ; " * and in describing his own procedure, he speaks after this fashion, " Christ whom we preach, warning every man and teaching every man, in all wisdom, that we may present every man perfect in Christ Jesus ; whereunto I also labor, striving according to his working, which worketh in me mightily." †

So also in the book of the Acts of the Apostles we observe, that in all their public discourses the first preachers of the Cross sought to carry conviction to the hearts of their hearers, and used every means to bring them to the acceptance of Christ, and to the beginning of a new life in Him. Now it is Peter on the day of Pentecost, or in the household of Cornelius ; and now it is Paul in the synagogue of Antioch, or on the top of Mars hill, and though like men well skilled in the reading of human nature, they varied their methods with the circumstances and previous histories of their audiences, yet always they had before them as their great aim the bringing of souls to Christ, and the carrying of them forward to higher attainments in Christ. Their constant design

---

* Ephesians iv. 11–13. † Colossians i. 28, 29.

was to move men to accept Him as their deliverer from sin, and to persuade them to adopt His precepts as the rule, and His example as the model of their lives. They endeavored everywhere to mold character through the presentation of "the truth as it is in Jesus." Or, as Paul himself has phrased it, they constantly attempted "by manifestations of the truth" to commend themselves "to every man's conscience, in the sight of God." *

In doing this, they did not care what happened to themselves. They had no eye or thought for anything but the benefit of their fellow-men through the proclamation of the gospel. Hardship might come upon them. They might be cast into prison or stoned till they were left for dead. But "none of these things moved them." They made objection only when men sought to worship them as gods. They did not measure their success by the applause they evoked, or by the comforts they secured, but only and always by the change which, through the power of God working with them, they produced upon their auditors. Not to display themselves, or to win for themselves the reputation of eloquence, did they labor. They could say to all the congregations which they addressed what Paul said to the Corinthians, "I seek not yours, but you;"† and their "joy and crown of rejoicing" was not in the preaching of sermons which might secure admiration, but rather in the winning of souls for Christ.

---

* 2 Corinthians iv. 2.   † 2 Corinthians xii. 14.

If they could succeed in that, they took joyfully the spoiling of their goods; and when, as at Ephesus, they saw conjurors renouncing their deeds of deceit and burning their books of magic, they had a reward which more than reconciled them to the "jeopardy" in which "every hour" they stood.

Now it is all-important that this one absorbing design of the Christian ministry, as illustrated so gloriously by the examples of those who were first invested with it, should be kept constantly before the mind of the preacher. For, partly owing to the public sentiment at present existing, and partly, also, to the necessary rhetorical training through which all candidates for the ministry must pass, there is great danger of our exalting that which is only a means, into the place which ought to be occupied by the end to which it is subordinate.

Among us everything runs to speech. The exercises of a commencement day are mainly "orations;" and eloquence at once opens the door to office and eminence, both in the State and in the Church. There is, besides, much that is gratifying to human pride, in being able to move large masses of people by the power of oratory. And so there is developed one of the perils of the modern pulpit. The preacher is tempted to aim at eloquence in itself, rather than at that, the gaining of which is the true evidence that he has been eloquent; and the doing of things according to strict rhetorical rule, is apt to be more accounted of than the securing of men's hearts for Christ, and the moving of them to strive after that holiness which he requires.* Now this is fatal, both as respects eloquence and as regards the impressing of our fellow-men. Oratory existed before rhetoric. He who succeeds in persuading another by the power of speech is, *ipso facto*, truly eloquent. And the rules of rhetoric have been generalized from the observation of the methods of those who have thus succeeded. It is very far from my object now to undervalue these deductions. On the contrary, they have a value in their own place which can hardly be overestimated. But that place is mainly for the pruning away of excrescences, and the correction of faults. They are good when you have thoroughly mastered them, but they are dreadfully pernicious when they have mastered you. So long as you are consciously speaking by rule, you will be hampered as really as if you were trying to walk in chains. You will be stilted, artificial, and unnatural. To strive after eloquence for the sake of being eloquent, will destroy eloquence. No man ever yet became great or effective in speech until he lost consciousness of himself, and of every-

---

* Mr. Spurgeon somewhere tells of a conversation between an eminent English surgeon and a French doctor, which may illustrate our meaning here. They were comparing notes regarding a certain very critical operation. The Frenchman averred that he had performed it more than three hundred times, while the Englishman said that he had attempted it only on eight occasions. "But how many did you save by it?" inquired the Englishman. "Oh, none at all!" was the answer; "but then the operation was brilliant!" "Ah!" replied the Englishman, "but I saved seven out of the eight." The salvation first! then let the brilliancy of the operation take care of itself.

thing else, in the one overmastering desire to move his hearers to adopt the course which he is advocating.*

Here, as in the kindred pursuits of art and music, comes in that gospel of unconsciousness which Carlyle in one of his essays has so characteristically expounded. "Moses wist not that the skin of his face shone while he talked with God,"† and evermore there is this same "wist not," when any one reaches the mountain-top of his peculiar power. He whose heart is so earnestly set on the salvation of men that he travails in birth of them "until Christ be formed in them," will, in addressing them, be eloquent, either according to rule, or in spite of rule, or above all rule; but he who is desirous mainly of following some scholastic precedent will degenerate into a pulpit pedant.

The effort to be eloquent will produce a rhetorician; the concentrated purpose to move men to live for God in Christ, will produce, in the end, an orator, and the

---

* The example of Mr. Jay, of Bath, in this respect, is most instructive. "I always found," says that preacher, "one thing very helpful in the choice and in the study of my subjects. It was the feeling of a rightness of aim and motive, *i. e.* a simple regard to usefulness, and a losing sight of advantage, popularity, and applause. This, it may be said, is rather a moral than an intellectual auxiliary. Be it so. But we know who has said, 'When thine eye is single thy whole body shall be full of light. And is not even reputation itself better and more surely acquired when it follows us, than when it is pursued?'"—*Jay's Autobiography, p.* 140.

† Exodus xxxiv. 29.

two are as far from each other as the poles.* Young men, "covet earnestly the best gifts, yet show I unto you a more excellent way." Seek men, not the reputation of eloquence or the incense of applause. Let your motto be the words of McAll, "I do not want heir admiration, I want their salvation;" and as you labor thus for their best interests, wrestling with God for them, and with them for God, you will be led to the best methods in a natural way, and eloquence will come before you are aware of it, bringing its attestation with it in the persons of those who have been, under God, transformed and transfigured by your instrumentality.

Thus again, we come round to the truth which I wish to strike as the key-note of these addresses, that SELF-RENUNCIATION IS THE ROOT OF EXCELLENCE. It is told of Pousa, the Chinese potter, that, being ordered to produce some great work for the emperor, he tried long to make it, but in vain. At length, driven to despair, he threw himself into the furnace, and the effect of his self-immolation on the ware, which was then in the fire, was such that it came out the most beautiful piece of porcelain ever known.† So in the Christian ministry, it is self-sacrifice that gives real excellence and glory to our work. When self in us disappears, and only Christ is seen,

---

* Paraphrasing the words of Professor Blackie, we might say here, "One may as well expect to make a great patriot of a fencing-master, as to make a great orator out of a mere rhetorician." See Blackie on Self-Culture, p. 18.

† See Harper's Magazine for September, 1875, p. 502.

then will be our highest success alike in our own lives and in the moving of our fellow-men.   We get near to the secret of Paul's greatness, when we hear him say, "According to my earnest expectation and my hope that Christ shall be magnified in my body, whether it be by life or by death ; " * and in the measure in which we imbibe his spirit, we shall rise to his efficiency. The worker, equally with the work, must be offered up in sacrifice to Christ, if at least the work is to be worthy of Him and of His cause.

---

* Philippians i. 20.

LECTURE II.

THE PREPARATION OF THE PREACHER.

LECTURE II.

THE PREPARATION OF THE PREACHER.

HAVING glanced at the nature and design of the work to which the preacher has consecrated himself, we are now ready to inquire what are the prerequisites to an efficient ministry.

And here, I take for granted that the preacher is himself a sincere and earnest Christian, and that he will constantly seek the co-operation with him of the Spirit of God. These are first principles with us; and, if I do not dwell upon them so fully as upon others which I shall presently name, do not suppose that I hold them to be less important. On the contrary, they are of the greatest moment. They are paramount and indispensable. But then, they are already recognized as such by you, for you are not here, I am persuaded, without having felt how essential these things are to the life and power of your ministry. At all events, if you have not that conviction, the kindest thing I can say to you is, "Go no farther until you get it."

It is only light that can enlighten. It is only fire that can kindle flame. Hence if we would illuminate others, we must have light in ourselves; and if we would kindle the flame of piety in the hearts of others, we must take the "live coal" with which we do so, from the burning "altar" of our own spirit. Even the heathen poet could say, "*Si vis me flere dolendum est primum ipsi tibi.*" If we be ourselves uninterested, how can we expect to interest others? if we be ourselves insincere, how can we hope to bring others to the faith? if we be ourselves cold, passionless, and dull, how can we expect to rouse others to enthusiasm?

But, even personal sincerity will not avail without the co-operation of the Holy Ghost, and so the connection between prayer in the closet and power in the pulpit is of the closest sort. He preacheth best who prayeth best. Prayer is to the minister what the minstrel's music was to Elisha, it prepares his soul for the descent of the Holy Ghost upon him, and where He is, there is power. Hence, the minister who neglects prayer, does, in his sermon, but lay Gehazi-like a cold staff upon the face of the dead; and there is no quickening result. It is only when, in the fullness of our love for souls, and in the boldness of our faith in God, we, as it were, stretch ourselves over them, and wrestle with Him on their behalf, that we become to them the conductors of new life. Ezekiel's prophesying produced a shaking among the bones, and an external readjustment of them each to each, but it was the breath of the Lord in answer to his prayer that gave them life. When, therefore, God pours out upon the minister the spirit of prayer, that is the prophecy of a coming revival in his church.

These are things most surely believed among us, and I have mentioned them now only that I may pre-

vent them from being consigned to what Coleridge*
has called "the dormitory of the soul," and may keep
them from lying bed-ridden there "side by side with
the most exploded errors."

But I do not dwell longer upon them now; neither
do I enlarge upon the necessity of that literary and
theological training which it is the proper business
of college and seminary to furnish. I would only say,
that in the interests of your future usefulness, you
will make a fatal mistake if you neglect to improve
to the fullest possible extent the advantages which
as students you here enjoy. Sometimes the temptation may suggest itself to you, that as your main
business in after-life will be that of preaching, you
may safely put your present class duties aside for the
purpose of devoting yourselves to preaching engagements. But such "raw haste" will be indeed "half-
sister to delay." What you gain in the matter of
practice will be more than lost in that of efficiency.
Of course, I do not object to your fulfilling those
appointments which may come in your way, provided
your doing so does not abstract your attention from
the work which you come here to perform. Give your
first care to the discharge of the seminary duties.
Fill up to the brim the ordinary channel of your
student-work, and then let the overflow, if there be
any, go to other engagements. This will be the true
economy in the end. You have facilities here, in the
shape of libraries, lectures, and advisors, the like of

---

* "Aids to Reflection." Aphorism I.

which in your after career you will never again enjoy.
Use them, therefore, to the utmost, and by doing so,
you will be " laying up for yourselves in store, a good
foundation against the time to come."

When you enter upon the work itself, you will find
that it will demand all your time and energies, and if
your lot should be cast, at length, in a large city with
its ceaseless demands upon you, there will be no little
difficulty felt by you in securing even so much seclusion as is required for the satisfactory preparation of
your weekly discourses; therefore, let this be your
gathering time. Lay everything in this institution
under tribute. Get the most you possibly can out of
every class. Master every subject that is brought before you ; and especially, master the original languages
in which the Word of God was given, so that you may
read them, not with the stammering hesitancy of one
who barely knows their alphabets, but with the critical appreciation of the scholar who recognizes the
minutest niceties in their construction. Continually
do I find myself in my work drawing upon the sav-
ings, if I may so express it, which I accumulated in
my student-life, and few regrets have been so bitter—
alas! that they are so unavailing—as those which I feel,
when I reflect, that if I had only been wiser in my generation then, I might have been much more useful and
efficient now. Therefore, though I presume not to
enter into the details of your studies, let me, from my
own experience, impress upon you the importance of
present devotion to your work here; for though
David, fresh from the sheep-fold, did such wonders

with his sling, every warrior is not a David, and for the average of men, it is better that they should submit to the drill and discipline which will make them expert in the use of ordinary weapons.

But, contenting myself thus with the merest reference to these things, I would give special and peculiar emphasis to *familiar acquaintance with the Scriptures*, as one of the most important prerequisites to pulpit power. You are to be ministers of the Word; and it is by the knowledge of the Scriptures that you are to be thoroughly furnished for your work.* The Bible is your text-book, and that not in the sense of being a hunting-ground for texts, but in that of constituting the ground-work of your discourses. You are looking forward to be "pastors and teachers," and the very thing which you are to teach is the Word of God. You are to lead your people up to an intelligent apprehension of its meaning, and a cordial reception of its statements, and it will be impossible for you to do that if you are not yourselves masters of its contents.

Moreover, the Bible is the great instrument of your power. The Spirit is *in* the word, as well as *with* the word. It carries its own evidence with it, and in the proportion in which you succeed in bringing your hearers face to face with its truthful and unflattering

---

* See 2 Tim. iii. 16, 17, where the furniture of the "man of God" is said by Paul to consist in a knowledge of the Holy Scriptures.

mirror, you will commend your utterances to their consciences in the sight of God. The great purpose of your office is to regenerate your hearers, and the one means which you are to employ for this, is "the Word of God which liveth and abideth forever." Herein you differ from those who are the exponents of a system of philosophy, and even from those who are the teachers of morality. Admirably has Bishop Wilberforce said, "That which is the object of philosophy is the accident of theology. It does not aim at answering speculative questions, doubts, and difficulties, though it does resolve them. It reveals the person of the Father, the Son, and the Holy Ghost, speaking at once to the highest reason; to that which apprehends by faith and not by the mere exercise of the logical faculty; to the will in its most secret recesses; and to all the affections in their highest sealed fountains." And again, "Incidentally it is the only real and efficient system of morality; but it is this only incidentally. Moral teaching by itself, with no insight and sanctions from without, from the true fountain-head of all being, is, amongst a fallen race, little better than mental and spiritual anatomy; a purblind poring into the nauseous revelations of disease and death; a groping darkly into the mechanism from which life has fled. Christianity is the bringing the mighty word of the Son of man to such an one, and saying in the strength of His Omnipotence to that dead corpse, 'Young man, I say unto thee, arise.'"*

---

* "Addresses to Candidates for Ordination," by the late Rt. Rev. Samuel Wilberforce, D.D., pp. 48, 49.

Now, this Christianity is revealed to us in the Scriptures of the Old and New Testaments—in the former, through type and prophecy; and in the latter, through history and exposition; if, therefore, we are to teach it correctly and preach it effectively, we must be thoroughly acquainted with these books. As he who is to practice the healing art must have, so to say, at his fingers' ends, the whole principles of medicine, and be perfectly familiar with the nature and effects of the remedies which he is to prescribe; or as he who gives himself to legal pursuits. should master the great authorities in his department; so the preacher of the gospel should be like Apollos, "mighty in the Scriptures."

Understand, therefore, that I am not now pressing upon you the duty of using the Word of God for the purpose of fostering habits of devotion in your own souls; though that, of course, you will not neglect. Neither am I enforcing upon you the importance of having your memories stored with its words, so that they may come at your bidding to strengthen and adorn your pulpit discourses. I am urging you to the systematic and continuous study of its books, that you may thoroughly familiarize yourselves with those truths in the proclamation of which your life-work is to consist. I wish you to have your minds so saturated with its spirit, that the first and most natural view you will take of any subject, will be the Biblical.

Form your system of theology from its pages. You cannot get on without having in your minds some systematic view of religious truth; but go to your system through the Bible, and beware of reading the Bible merely through the spectacles of system. Be the slaves of no system; but be always the docile disciples of the Word of God. That was an all-important distinction which Whately drew, when he said: "A desire to have Scripture on our side, is one thing; the desire to be on the side of Scripture is quite another." Be it yours to find out which is the side of Scripture, and determine always to take that. Mark very carefully the perspective in which it places different truths, and when you preach these truths, be sure always to put them in the same relative position as that in which you found them in its pages.

Read it as a whole, that you may have a comprehensive survey of its contents. Read it inductively, that you may gather together into so many different centres all its utterances on particular matters of doctrine or duty.* Read it book by book, that you may discover the drift and purpose of each separate contribution which, under the guidance of the Spirit, each writer has made to its aggregate unity. Resolve that whatever else you read or leave unread, you will

---

* As specimens of the kind of induction to which I here refer, let me mention the works of Smeaton and Crawford on the Atonement; and as treating the same subject in a similar manner, but on a different principle of classification, the recent volume of Mr. Dale, of Birmingham. In this connection, also, I would direct attention to some of the sermons of Thomas Binney, in the volume entitled "Sermons preached in the King's Weigh-house Chapel, London, 1829–1869." Macmillan & Co., 1869.

at least master that which is for you professionally, as well as experimentally, THE BOOK. And never imagine that you have perfectly possessed yourselves of all its treasures; for, ever as you grow in intellectual vigor and in Christian experience, you will find that you have grown into the capacity of discovering just so much the more in its treatises and narratives, its sermons and its songs.

When I was a student of theology, a cursory remark dropped by one of my beloved tutors, to the effect that "we read far too much about the Bible, and far too little in the Bible," was for me a word in season. It set me to such study of the Scriptures as I am now enforcing upon you, and if God has given me any measure of usefulness in my ministry, not a little of it has been due to my determination to become "well-instructed in the oracles of God." Other attainments were beyond my reach. I had not the means of pursuing studies in many departments which were open to my more fortunate contemporaries; but this was at my hand, and so I gave myself to it, and for years I have been in the habit of gauging my mental growth by the clearer apprehension which I have gained of some portion of the Scriptures, than I had at the time when it was last under my consideration.

You will see, therefore, that the acquaintance with the Word of God which I am recommending to you, is not that of the letter merely. I do not mean that you are to become such prodigies of memory, that if the whole Bible were to be destroyed, you could easily restore it. Neither do I wish you to be walking concordances, able at a moment's notice to give the chapter and the verse of every quotation that may be made in your hearing. What I desire is, that you should become as familiar with its modes of presenting the truth, as you are with the text-books of your classes. And if you will be advised from my experience, I would urge you to make your study of it at first hand, and for yourselves. You will find many hand-books offered for your assistance, and many analyses of its teachings pressed upon your attention. But, in the first instance at least, *make your own*. For while you are prosecuting your investigation for one purpose, you will incidentally, and by the way, pick up a great many valuable things which otherwise you might never have seen. Besides, that which you discover for yourself, remains with you a permanent possession, while that which you take readymade from the labors of another, is very speedily forgotten. " Search the Scriptures " then, my young brethren. It is an old injunction, but it is as important now as it was centuries ago. " Read, mark, learn, and inwardly digest " them, and you will grow into an efficiency as preachers which you could not otherwise acquire.

Not without its lesson in this regard is that marvelous spiritual movement which within the last two years has stirred Great Britain to its depths, as it has never been since the days of Whitefield and the Wesleys, and which has begun under the same instrumentality in our own land. Here are plain, unlettered men, in many respects open to criticism in their meth-

ods, yet blessed to the revival of multitudes, and to
the conversion of still greater numbers; and when
you come to analyze their power—so far as it can be
submitted to mere human analysis—much of it is
found to consist in the fact, that they are skilled in
the use of that Word of God, which is "quick and
powerful, sharper than any two-edged sword, piercing
even to the dividing asunder of soul and spirit, and
of the joints and marrow, and is a discerner of the
thoughts and intents of the hearts." * Let us learn
from their example. Let us not prefer the "wisdom
of words" to its words of wisdom. Let us teach our
people to bow before its utterances, by the reverence which we ourselves manifest in its treatment.
Yea, let us recognize the signs of the times in this
particular, and as everywhere the people are hungering for the Word, and do eagerly welcome it when it
is faithfully and lovingly expounded to them, let us
furnish ourselves for the demand that is thus made
upon us, by gathering daily of its heavenly manna.

Another prerequisite to success in the pulpit is *a
good knowledge of the human heart*. The physician
must understand, not merely the nature of the remedies which he is to employ, but also the symptoms
and workings of the diseases which he desires to cure.
He must "walk the hospitals" as well as study the
pharmacopeia. Now, the gospel is a remedial measure, and therefore it is essential that its preachers

---

* Hebrews iv. 12.

should be acquainted with the nature of man, as well as with the means which, as the instrument in the hands of God's spirit, he is to use for its transformation and renewal. Hence, he who wishes to become an efficient minister, will be a diligent student of men.

Begin here with yourselves; for " as face answereth to face in a glass, so doth the heart of man to man." There are distinctive peculiarities, indeed, in each individual, but in their great outstanding characteristics, men everywhere are very much alike. Therefore you may safely take it for granted, that what you find in your own hearts, exists also in those of others. The burden of guilt which weighed so heavily on your consciences, will be found pressing also upon theirs, if only you can succeed in bringing them to that knowledge of God's law by which you were awakened to a sense of your sinfulness. The blood of Christ which cleansed you from your iniquities, will be as efficacious also in their cases, if they will apply it to themselves in simple faith. The struggle which you have continually to carry on with the evil principles that are yet within you, must be maintained also by them, and whatever is felt by you to be helpful in that holy war, will be welcomed, you may be sure, by them. The besetments which encircle you, will in some form or other environ them; the weaknesses which you feel so frequently, and in consequence of which you yield so often to temptation, will be felt by them; and whatever has been to you the means of revival, will certainly prove restorative to them. The limitations within which you have to carry on

your labor on the earth, and which mar so much the
symmetry and completeness of your work, will be
similar to those which they have often felt so galling
to them, and everything which has tended to sustain
and comfort you under your humiliation, will be
equally valuable to them.   They have their unsettle-
ments and trials in life just as you have; they have
their emptyings from "vessel to vessel" just as you
have; they have their sorrows, and sicknesses, and
bereavements just as you have; and by telling them
how you have been upborne, you "may be able to
comfort them that are in any trouble, by the comfort
wherewith you yourselves are comforted of God." *

Thus alike in the matter of warning and in that of
consolation, you will find that a strict watch over your
own hearts and histories will give you signal power.
The conflict with, and conquest over, one single bosom
sin, will give you here an influence which you will
seek in vain from any other quarter.   Peter could
never have written his first Epistle, which is so full
of comfort to them who "are in heaviness through
manifold temptations," if he had not himself known
what it was to hang through days of darkness on
the memory of his Master's loving look.   And those
are ever the most effective preachers to others who
are speaking from their knowledge of their own hearts.

On the day on which I was licensed as a preacher
of the gospel, my father, who was then suffering from
the disease of which he died, repeated to me a sen-

---

* 2 Corinthians i. 4.

tence which fifty years before he had heard in the
charge given at an ordination by an old pastor to
the newly-installed minister. It was to this effect:
"Preach to the hearts of your hearers, and that you
may do that effectively, examine well your own heart,
and whatever you find there, charge home upon them."
Perhaps the circumstances in which this advice was
repeated to me, tended to give it more importance
than it really deserves. Yet, I am free to say, that it
has very seldom been absent from my thoughts when
I have been preparing for the pulpit; and sometimes,
when some one of my hearers has alleged that I was
preaching most pointedly *at* him, I was, in reality,
preaching most solemnly to myself; while on other
occasions, I have been made the messenger of consolation to many, when I was seeking most earnestly
for my own comfort.

The poet has said that "one touch of nature makes
the whole world akin," and a minister thrills his hearers most when they feel his nature touching theirs.
There is something in the eye of a well-painted portrait which makes every beholder think that it is
looking at him, and that no matter at what point he
stands. Now, this speaking from his own heart will
give a similar power to the sermon of the preacher,
and will make every hearer feel that it was meant for
him. Know yourselves, then, and use that knowledge
as a key for opening the hearts of others to your
words. Let your own hearts and consciences always
form a portion of your audience, and if you are affected, others will be also.

Have you observed how when God has called His greatest servants to some signal service, He has begun by giving them a thorough revelation of themselves, through the unveiling of Himself to them? Now it is Moses* at the burning bush, and when he has discovered his imperfections, the commission is given, "Go, and I will be with thy mouth and teach thee what thou shalt say." Now it is Gideon† at the threshing-floor, and when he has said, "O my Lord, wherewith shall I save Israel, behold my family is poor in Manasseh, and I am the least in my father's house;" he is then in a fit state to receive the command, "Go, in this thy might." Now it is Isaiah‡ in the Temple filled with the glory of Jehovah, and when he has found out that he is "a man of unclean lips," and has received purification by fire from the altar, he is ready to offer himself to the call of the Lord, with the words of dedication, " Here am I, send me!" Now it is Peter,§ on the shore of Gennesaret, seeing the glory of the Lord through the miracle of the fishes, and crying, "Depart from me, for I am a sinful man, O Lord," and then he is prepared for the reassuring words, "Fear not, from henceforth thou shalt catch men." The knowledge of his own heart, through and along with an experimental acquaintance with Christ — *these* are the mightiest elements of the preacher's power. I have seen a housemaid in one of our great hotels, take a

---

* Exodus iv. 10.   † Judges vi. 11–15.

‡ Isaiah vi. 1–8.   § Luke v. 1–16.

skeleton-key and pass into every chamber in a spacious corridor, laying open the contents of each, and setting to work on its purification. Now, such a skeleton-key is the knowledge of his own heart to the minister of Christ. It enables him to unlock the hearts of his hearers and enter into them, and turn out their hidden things, so that they cry, "Who told him all that? he seems to be reading out the innermost secrets of my soul." Who told him? It was Jesus, in the day when His divine light flashed into his soul, and let him see himself!

But in this matter of the knowledge of human nature, you will also gain much advantage from the study of the biographies which the Word of God contains. The history of the first temptation is repeated in every enticement to sin still, and the weaknesses even of such men as Abraham and Moses, Aaron and Elijah, Peter and Thomas, are continually reappearing among ourselves. Everywhere we may find those who, like Balaam, "love the wages of unrighteousness," while they seek to obey the letter of the divine precept. Daily we are meeting with men whose great difficulty, when we urge them to a certain course, is that of the Jewish king, who said to the man of God, "But what shall we do for the hundred talents which I have given to the army of Israel?"* and the class whom Demetrius so moved when he said, "Sir, ye know that by this craft we have our wealth,"† is not by any means extinct among us. There are too many

---

* 2 Chron. xxv. 9.   † Acts xix. 25.

still like Herod,* who are " very sorry, yet," for the sake of some fancied obligation to party, or to promise, go and do what their consciences condemn. We have yet our Diotrepheses,† who "love to have the pre-eminence among the brethren," as well as our Aquilas and Priscillas, who are our "helpers in Christ Jesus." But why need I enumerate individual instances? You will find in the characters described in the Bible representatives of every phase of human nature presently existing among ourselves, and so, if you wish to furnish yourselves fully for dealing with men in the momentous matter of the salvation of their souls, you will study well the portrait gallery of the Book of God.

Let each biography here be to you a matter of separate analysis, and let each character be regarded by you as the type of a class, specimens of which you are sure to meet with in your after lives. This will prepare you for the actual work of the ministry, not only by suggesting to you fruitful themes for your public discourses, but also by familiarizing you with the doublings and deceitfulnesses of that human heart, with which, as the preachers of the Gospel, you will have especially to do.

In this department, also, you may be greatly benefited by the diligent study of the characters which are described in human literature. The pages of history will give you ample materials for coming to a decision as to the motives by which men in general

* Mark vi. 26. † 3 John 9; Romans xvi. 3.

are actuated; for though the transactions which are there described are larger and more important than those in which the average of mankind are engaged, yet the principles by which they who took part in them were animated, are the same as those which are acted upon by the majority of men in the ordinary affairs of life.

But better, perhaps, than any history, for the end which I am now setting before you, are the dramatic works of Shakespeare. To them, I, at least, must acknowledge my obligations, in the most emphatic manner. They came into my hands during my second session at the University of Glasgow, and opened up what was virtually a new world to me. For more than two years I devoted to them every minute of my leisure time. I read them not for the sake of the stories which they told, or the plots which they unravelled, but for the insight which they gave me into the workings of the human heart. I was especially fascinated with those plays which manifest the power of conscience; and long before I knew of the writings of Schlegel and Coleridge, I had made for myself an analysis of the characters of Macbeth, Richard III., Brutus, Hamlet, Iago, and others. The productions were crude enough, no doubt; yet, the mere attempt at such work was valuable to me beyond most other things; and to this day I look back with no ordinary pleasure on the hours which I spent in such a delightful manner.

It is not without a measure of trepidation, indeed, that I venture to mention this, for I have still vividly before my mind the consternation of my father, a worthy elder in the Presbyterian Church, when he discovered the nature of my studies at that time. Sitting up one evening until far past midnight at my favorite pursuits, I happened to burst into a long, loud laugh over a ludicrous passage which I was reading, and to make some noise by the movement of my chair. This disturbed my venerable parent in his slumbers, for my room was immediately over his, and in a few minutes I was confronted with the vision of a man in white, who, on finding out how I was engaged, very gravely said to me, " My man, if you are going to preach Christ's Gospel, you had better be doing something else at this time in the morning than reading a play-actor's books." I fear, therefore, lest some exemplary Christian people may think that I am giving you perilous advice, when I recommend you to make yourselves familiarly acquainted with the characters which the great dramatist has so powerfully depicted. But I am reassured when I remember that if I err here, I err in good company, since I find that Dr. Guthrie wrote, " I never tire of reading Shakespeare. I have always considered him the greatest uninspired genius that ever lived ; and I remember how glad I was when reading the biography of Dr. Chalmers, to find that he was of the same mind."* In spite, therefore, of the prejudice which many friends entertain against the class of works to which Shakespeare's

---

* Autobiography and Memoir of Thomas Guthrie, D.D. Vol. II., p. 310.

writings belong, I would urge you to make a study of these noble productions, for though occasionally you will meet with some things which indicate that according to his own plaintive confession, his nature had become "subdued to that it wrought in, like the dyer's hand."* Yet every candid critic must agree with Sir James Stephens when he says,† "In his soul, as in a mirror, were concentrated all the lights radiating from every point of human observation, and from his soul as from a mirror these lights were reflected back in every possible combination of beauty and sublimity, of wisdom and wit, of pathos and humor."

But while you avail yourselves of all these means of acquiring a knowledge of human nature, do not forget to mingle much among men themselves. Keep your eyes and ears open wherever you are, whether in the streets, or in the cars, in the exchange, in the stores, or in the household, and be closely observant of everything which indicates or illustrates character. Seek to become acquainted with persons in every profession and pursuit, and study especially the temptations to which they are most open, and the weaknesses which they most commonly manifest in their ordinary avocations. Beware, however, of prosecuting such investigations in a spirit of cynicism like that which comes out in the pages of *Vanity Fair;* or with a view to the pro-

---

* See his cxi. Sonnet.

† Lecture on Desultory and Systematic Reading, by the Rt. Hon. Sir James Stephen, p. 25.

duction of such comic effects as those which have
made the cartoons of *Punch* so famous. You stand
upon a higher platform than that of the moralist or
the satirist.   Your mission is to be the helpers of
your fellow-men into the life of peace and purity
which Christ has revealed to them and made possible
for them, and therefore all your observations must be
made with a benevolence like that which " stirred "
the spirit of the apostle when he passed through the
streets of Athens, and marked how the city was
" wholly given to idolatry,"* and with the view of
leading them as he did, from the very inscriptions on
their own idol-altars, up to the knowledge of the Lord
Jesus.

We can never hope to reach the excellence of the
Redeemer Himself, yet it may not be irreverent to
say here, that one of the sources of His power as a
preacher, lay in the fact that " He knew what was in
men." †   He had " the tongue of the learned " that
He should " know how to speak a word in season to him
that is weary." ‡ Hence, there was a perfect adaptation
in His words to the characters and circumstances of His
hearers.   To some He would not fully " commit Himself;" and He had one way of presenting His message
to the formal Pharisee, and another to the weeping
penitent. He brought the same salvation to the ruler
Nicodemus, and to the woman at the well of Sychar,
but He approached each in the way that was best
suited to gain His end with each; while in His public

---

* Acts xvii. 16.   † John ii. 24, 25.   ‡ Isaiah l. 4.

addresses He rose with perfect naturalness from the occupations of men's daily lives to the contemplation of things unseen and eternal. He called men at the receipt of customs to "follow" Him, and they obeyed by leaving their occupations and attending Him through His journeyings. It is ours to go to them still in their business pursuits, and persuade them to follow Him, while yet they sit at their accustomed work. So the nearer we can attain to that acquaintance with the human heart which He possessed, the more effective ever will be our appeals. In Him that knowledge was the omniscience of godhead, but in us it must be laboriously acquired by the observation of our fellows.

To this then, gentlemen, give yourselves with all your earnestness. There is a way to every man's heart if you can only find it. Study him, therefore, until you discover it, and then enter in by it, and take possession of him for your Lord. Let him feel and know that you come to assist him in his conflict with himself; that you are in alliance with those aspirations after something higher and nobler than he is, which are the strongest yearnings of his heart; that you are desirous of helping him to withstand those temptations with which every day he has to contend, and you will gain not his ear only, but his heart, almost before he is aware of it.

On my way to the pulpit, and as a means of self-help, I spent a year in the editorial chair of a newspaper; and I question if any of my college classes was more valuable to me, so far as my after life-work has been concerned, than the experience of dealing

with men which I then obtained. If anybody wants
to know human nature, all round, within and without, and through and through, let him be for a time
the editor of a newspaper! and if, as was the case
with me, a contested election should happen to occur
during his term of office, he will have ample opportunity of studying every variety of character!

I was helped in this department also, by some time
devoted to public teaching, a work in which the
monotony of the class was varied by watching the
peculiarities of the children, and sometimes, too, by
the opportunity it gave of insight into the petty ambitions and schemings of the parents. And though
these observations were made in another land, I have
not found that human nature in New York is different from that which manifests itself in Scotland.

My advice to you in this matter, then, my young
brethren, is that you should avail yourselves of every
opportunity which offers itself, in your various engagements, for the study of your fellow-men. Be
always taking notes, without seeming to do so, and
let the results of your observations shape your public
discourses. It makes little or no difference how you
acquire it ; only somehow get a knowledge of your
fellows, so that when you preach to them, you shall
not seem to them like " one who beateth the air,"
but may speak as one who knows the difficulties with
which they have to contend, and the dangers by
which they are environed. " When I listen to some
preachers," said a ship-builder on the Tyne once, to a
minister of my acquaintance, " I can build a whole

ship; but this morning I declare I could not lay a single plate." " How was that?" asked my friend. " Because," was the reply, " you spoke like one who knew just what I needed, and I could not withdraw my attention from you for a moment." That is the sort of sermons which a knowledge of human nature and daily life, rightly applied, will enable you to preach, and which you ought always to try to preach. For I do not think that merchants, or indeed, for that matter, any class of busy, struggling men or women, receive nearly as much sympathy, encouragement, or assistance from the pulpit as they ought. The discourses they hear may be good enough as theological discussions, or as moral essays, or as beautiful illustrations of some little facet of truth, but they do not, nearly so often as they should, touch the inner histories and experiences of men, living as we are doing now, and the reason is because the preacher is too frequently a respectable recluse, knowing little or nothing of the battle which human souls are daily fighting, in their homes, in the streets, or in their stores. Study men, therefore. Find out the "weights" by which they are hindered in their daily race, and the dangers to which they are most liable. Then preach so that the wave of your speech shall flow into their hearts and lift them up above the sandbanks on which the work of the week had left them stranded, and you will never be without their attention. Nay, as the week advances, they will long for the recurrence of the Sabbath that they may be strengthened through your ministry once more, and when the service is

ended they will retire with the feeling that in spite
of the down-dragging influences that are depressing
them, there is something worth striving for after all,
and with the resolution that they will begin anew to
live for Christ.

It is true, indeed, that as ministers, you will be yourselves removed from the sphere of many of the difficulties with which men in business have to contend ;
but your very exemption from these will enable you
the better to help them, provided you know enough
about them. As described by Mr. MacGregor, in one
of his " Rob Roy " books,* the process of adjusting
the compasses on board ship in the river Thames, is
something like this : The vessel is moored in the
bight at Greenhithe, and by means of warps to certain government buoys, she is placed with her head
towards the various points of the compass, one after
another. The bearing of her compass on board, in-
fluenced as that is by the attraction of the iron she
carries, is taken accurately by one observer in the
vessel, and the true bearing is signalled to him by
another observer on shore, who has a compass out of
reach of the local attraction of the ship. The error
in each position is thus ascertained, and the necessary
corrections are made. Now in the church your people
are like that observer on board ship. Their consciences have been all the week affected by the influence of things immediately around them, so that

---

* The reference is to " The Voyage Alone In The Yawl Rob
Roy," but I have not the volume at hand and cannot quote the
page.

they are in danger of making serious mistakes even in their reading of the book of God. But in the pulpit, you are like the observer on shore. You are away from the magnetic agencies—mostly metallic— which so seriously affect them, therefore you can signalize to them their " true bearings," and thus prepare them for the voyage of the week that is to follow. You can read the directions of God's Word with an unbiased mind, while from your acquaintance with their circumstances, you will know what directions they need for their daily guidance. Get such a knowledge, my young brethren, on the one hand of the book of God, and on the other of the characters and surroundings of men, as will enable you thus to be of service to them, just where they are, and you may be sure that you will always have numerous, interested, and grateful hearers.

LECTURE III.

THE PREPARATION OF THE PREACHER—CONTINUED.

LECTURE III.

THE PREPARATION OF THE PREACHER, CONTINUED.

AMONG those things which are needed to the furnishing of a successful preacher, I would give an important place to the *study of the works of standard authors.* Paul said to Timothy, "Give attendance to reading," and the advice is even more needed in modern times than it was in the days in which he lived, for now "many are running to and fro, and knowledge has been increased." If the minister is to be a leader of men, he must keep ahead of them, or at least abreast with them in ordinary intelligence, for, if they detect him blundering in matters of history, philosophy, or literature, or if they discover that he is comparatively ignorant in these departments, they will have little respect for his opinions and small confidence in his judgment, even when he is speaking to them of things that lie within his proper province.

But, over and above this negative advantage, the effort to master the writings of great thinkers will strengthen your own minds, while the truths which they proclaim, will suggest to you trains of thought which otherwise might never have occurred to you. Absolute originality, nowadays, is all but an impossibility The most we can hope for is that we shall be able to give freshness and point to our own thinking, as we go over the subjects on which men have exercised their intellects from the beginning until now; and, for my part, I know no method by which that can be secured more thoroughly than by the wise use of good books.

Some, indeed, have affected to despise their assistance, but the result of such a course is, in most instances, mental barrenness. We all know how stimulating it is to come into contact with a great man. His talk is extraordinarily helpful. There is that in his words which makes them seminal and germinant, so that they take root in our minds and spring up, and bring forth fruit which is a joy to us, and a benefit to those with whom we share it. But a similar effect is produced in the diligent student by a great book. In reading such a production we are, as it were, listening for the time to the conversation of its author, on those subjects on which he was most at home, and we become possessed of that which if he had been questioned regarding it, he would have valued more highly than all his other attainments : thus, pigmies though we may be ourselves, in perusing the writings of those standard thinkers who have enriched the world with their works, we stand on the shoulders of earth's intellectual giants, and behold all that was visible to their searching gaze. Cultivate an acquaintance, therefore, with good books ; for as one has beautifully said : " They are the masters who instruct us without rods or anger ; if you approach them, they are not asleep ; if you inquire of them,

they do not hide themselves; they do not chide if
you err; they do not laugh if you are ignorant. It
matters not in what mood we are, they are ever the
same; Milton's Paradise knows no winter; and the
bells of Bunyan's New Jerusalem are always ringing
joy." *

But you cannot read every book, and it would not
be desirable that you should do so, even if you could.
Here, therefore, selection is necessary, and for making
that, no better direction can be given you than that
addressed the other day by Dean Stanley to the students of the University of St. Andrews : " Read the
great books, and let the little ones take care of
themselves." Richard Cecil said : " I have a shelf in
my study for tried authors ; one in my mind for tried
principles, and one in my heart for tried friends."
Now there are certain tried books, which by common
consent have been placed apart from all others in our
language, and elevated to a quasi-peerage in our literature ; and these you ought to study, not through the
medium of abridgments or other make-shifts, but in
the original productions. What these are will immediately suggest themselves to you in connection with
the departments to which they severally belong, and
I will not stay to attempt to enumerate them ; but I
may say that it would not be creditable to any minister using our mother tongue, if he were ignorant of
Shakespeare and Milton among the poets ; Gibbon,

---

* Religion : Its Influence on the Working Man at his Leisure,
a Lecture by Rev. William Graham, Liverpool, p. 9.

Macaulay, and Motley among the historians; Locke, Reid, Hamilton, and Mill among the philosophers; or Butler, Edwards, and Chalmers among the theologians. While in the various branches of natural science, after having made yourselves familiar with the elements, you will find it of advantage to go at once to the writings of those who are the acknowledged masters in each.

But never forget that the manner of your reading is as important as the matter. Samuel Johnson used to say, "Whatever is worth doing at all is worth doing well." And if a book be worth reading at all, it should be perused with care and attention. Simple, however, as this statement looks, many never act upon it. They are mere devourers of books, and so suffer from literary dyspepsia. They never attempt to digest and assimilate the thoughts of others, for their one care seems to be to get over the pages, so that they may add another to the list of works which they can say they have read. And there are multitudes more, who do not give even so much attention to them as that. They glance over the preface, read hurriedly the table of contents, dip here and there into the work itself, and then go away professing that they understand the whole. Dean Swift complained of some, in his day, that they did with books what others did with great Lords in the peerage, namely, learned their titles, and then went away and boasted of their acquaintance; and it is to be feared that not a few are guilty of the same pretensiveness in our own times. Let it not be so with you. When you take up a work, resolve to understand it thoroughly. The ancients had a proverb — *Cave hominem unius libri* (Beware of the man of one book)—in which they noted that he who had perfectly mastered one book was a tougher antagonist by far than the mere *helluo librorum*, who "bolts" books by the dozen, as a Dorset laborer "bolts bacon." Thomas Fuller has quaintly said, "I judge of good housekeeping not by the number of chimneys, but by the smoke." So you may gauge your intellectual strength not by the number of books which you have perused, but by that of those which you have digested and made your own. One standard author, pored over until he has become a part of ourselves, will do more for the cultivation of our minds than a whole library superficially glanced at.

And that you may know what I mean by thorough reading, let us take the case of such a work, for example, as "Butler's Analogy." As you lift the volume, you must be warned not to expect that you have an easy task before you. There is very little that is pleasing in the style, and there is much that is intricate and involved in the argument, so that you must keep yourselves constantly alert, and make every sentence a study. But if you will only prosecute your investigation with wisdom and perseverance to the end, you will rise from the perusal of that book with a sense of satisfaction such as rarely fills the soul. No doubt authors, since Butler's day, have so drunk into his spirit and developed his views, that, unconsciously to ourselves, we have on many subjects been breathing the atmosphere which he created, and this may prevent us from having the same sense of novelty in the study of the "Analogy" as those must have felt who first read its pages, but still, he was to ethics and Christian evidences almost what Bacon and Newton were to the physical sciences; and much that is best in our moral philosophy and theology for the past hundred years, is but the development of "way-side seeds" which fell from his full hand as he went forth to sow in the field which he had chosen. But, more than most other books, the "Analogy" is a study, and to master it thoroughly, you must take it by degrees. Read a chapter at a time, carefully marking on the margin the various steps of the closely-compacted argument, and at the close comparing your own analysis with the summary which he himself gives at the end of each section. In this work, as well as in weighing the precise force or estimating the legitimateness of his several arguments, you may receive some useful hints from the notes in Bishop Fitzgerald's admirable edition, and also from the criticisms of Chalmers on each chapter, which are to be found in one of the volumes of his posthumous works. Thus furnished, you will make your way slowly, but surely, along; and when you reach the end, you will have become so accustomed to the style and method of reasoning, that you will be able to return and reperuse the earlier portions of the work, not only with ease, but also with positive enjoyment. Such a book, so studied, will make a man a thinker, and "set him up" in philosophy and theology for life.

Other examples might be given, but this must suffice ; and, from my own experience, I feel warranted in saying that, if you will only set about something of this kind, with some of our standard books, it will do more for you in the way of furnishing you with mental strength for the pulpit than all the education of all the schools.*   I do not prescribe any particular method, only let it be understood to be essential that in some way meditation should be secured along with reading. What mastication and digestion are to food, in the process of the nourishment of the body, that meditation is to reading, in the development of the mind.   Hence it was a good rule which was given by a scholar to a friend,† " Proportion an hour's reflection to an hour's reading, and so dispirit the book into the student."   And your own Dr. Dwight often said that the weakness of his eye-sight was attended with this advantage, that it compelled him to think much.

It is a good plan to compare notes on your read-

---

* To those who wish more minute directions on this subject, I would recommend the lecture of Dr. Channing on " Self-Culture," to be found in his collected works ; also the recent valuable little book of Professor Blackie, of Edinburgh, on " Self-Culture," and the exhaustive and every way admirable treatise of President Porter on " Books and Reading."   Willmott's " Pleasures, Objects, and Advantages of Literature," though sketchy and in some degree fragmentary, is often very suggestive ; and the chapter on Books in Mr. Emerson's " Society and Solitude" is full of nuggets of the purest gold.

† Willmott, as above, page 38.

ing with a brother, like-minded with yourself, and so in your daily walks you may combine the advantages of physical exercise with those of mental culture. In the early years of my Liverpool pastorate, I was greatly beholden to a beloved friend, still in the ministry in that town, whose fine taste, extensive information, boundless humor, and kindly heart made our weekly conference along the shore of the Mersey a stimulus and a joy to me. Reading had made him a full man, and conference a ready man. I dare not add that writing had made him an exact man; but he was to me one of the best of teachers, for he let me see how to get at the kernel of a book without breaking my teeth upon the shell.*

But if, from the isolation of your position, you cannot have such brotherly assistance from another, then talk to yourself on the subject with your pen. Write a criticism of your own upon your author, and if you think him wrong on any point, try your strength against him, in the shape of an exposure of his error, and an enforcement of that which you believe to be the truth. This will be a capital intellectual exercise, even if no human eye should ever see your essay but your own; while, perhaps, the sending of it to your author,† or the giving of it to the press in some

---

* The reference here is to my much-loved brother, the Rev. William Graham, whose fellowship for sixteen years was one of the dearest privileges of my life.

† The publication of his essay on the " Philosophy of the Infinite," in which, while yet a student, he criticised the system of Sir William Hamilton, has resulted in the elevation of Professor

periodical, may often furnish stimulus or give direction to your whole after-career. But, *quocunque modo*, anyhow, compel yourself to think on what you read, if you would make your reading minister to your pulpit efficiency.

The remarks which I have just made have prepared the way for the announcement of the next prerequisite to ministerial efficiency on which I would insist, namely, *the free and constant use of the pen in the work of original composition.* I enter not now on the consideration of such questions as whether sermons should be written, and if so, whether they should be read from the manuscript or delivered *memoriter* or otherwise; these will come up at a later stage; meanwhile, however it is to be with your preparations for the pulpit in after-days, I am disposed to insist upon it as positively essential to your success, that you should now acquire facility in writing. I do not care very much what subjects you may treat, or what the immediate object may be which you have in view, only I would urge it upon you with all the emphasis

---

Calderwood to the chair of Moral Philosophy in Edinburgh; and for the sake of the lesson which it points, I may be forgiven for saying that the writing, while I was but a youth of nineteen, of a review of an article which had appeared in the *Journal of Sacred Literature*, and the sending of it to Dr. John Kitto, while he was the editor of that Quarterly, was my first entrance into the field of authorship. I wrote it for my own improvement, and sent it to him by the advice of others, much against my own inclination; but when I saw it in actual type, the very letters danced before my eyes!

I can command, that you should accustom yourselves to composition.

This will give definiteness and precision to your thinking. What you can write on any subject is really all that you know concerning it, and the character of your composition will infallibly indicate the quality of your knowledge. The pen is a wonderful crystallizer, and if the work of meditation be sufficiently advanced, its employment will be all that is needed to give solidity and arrangement to your thoughts. If, however, your ideas are crude and ill-digested, your composition will be hazy and disjointed, and you will be tempted to make up for the lack of more valuable materials by the importation into it of high-sounding verbiage. Thus you may test with unerring accuracy the completeness of your thinking by the character of your style. When your words are clear, simple, strong, you are treading on ground with which you are familiar; when your language is vague, indefinite, and obscure, you may depend upon it that you have not yet attained to a thorough understanding of your subject. Hence, even as a means of study, the use of the pen is indispensable.

But copious composition is also valuable as ministering to readiness of expression. As preachers, you will have to discourse week by week to your hearers. Now whether your sermons are to be written or spoken merely from careful thinking beforehand, you will equally need facility in the art of clothing your ideas in words. If you write your discourses, then you will never get through your work, if you should proceed, as his friends used jokingly to say John Foster did, at the rate of a sentence a day. If, again, you are to speak from premeditation merely, then, unless you have acquired the habit of easily giving verbal shape to your thoughts, you will be hesitating and hampered in your utterance, or you will be borne along by a fatal fluency, in which reiteration will take the place of argument, and sound will be made to serve for sense. The only preventive against these dangers lies in acquiring the habit of giving definite expression to your thoughts by frequent composition. It will not come of itself. It is the result of practice, for, as Pope has said :

> "True ease in writing comes from art, not chance,
> As those move easiest who have learned to dance."

Let the pen, therefore, be always in your hand, or at your hand, and seek to acquire the art of expression so thoroughly that when you have a thought to utter, the language appropriate for its communication will come to you as naturally as, when you are writing a word, the letters required for the spelling of it rise to your remembrance.

Aim at the securing of a style which shall present your thoughts forcibly, clearly, and eloquently to the minds of your hearers; and do not suppose that you can accomplish that without long and laborious practice. Cultivate acquaintance with the writings of those who have been famous for this peculiarity; for, as one can acquire the manners of

good society only by mixing in it, so we can catch
the ease and elegance of a good style only by reading first-rate authors.   I do not mean, of course, that
you are to imitate them in your compositions, but
merely that from the insensible influence of their
example upon you, their beauty and simplicity may
repeat themselves through you.   No one will charge
John Bright with imitation.   He is the most natural
of orators; and yet, when we are told that for many
years he has been in the habit, before retiring to rest
after the excitement of a night in the House of Commons, of reading for an hour from one of the poets,
taking a new one each winter, and that he has thus
gone over most of the classic poetry of his native
land, we think we have discovered one of the factors
which have gone to produce that wonderful combination of simplicity and power, of beauty and
strength, by which his speeches are distinguished.

Seek to get the best words and to put them in the
best places.   Yet do not suppose that the biggest are
necessarily the best.   The vice of much of the writing
in these days in newspapers, periodicals, and even in
sermons, is pretensiveness.   The authors are ambitious
to show their learning, and common words, which are
common simply because they are the most expressive
and intelligible, are treated as if they were vulgar, and
forced to give place to others which have nothing but
their learned origin or their unusual length to recommend them.   Remember that in every sort of composition perspicuity is more than half the battle, and
that a meaning which does not stare a man in the

face is as bad as no meaning at all, since he will most likely never trouble himself to attempt to discover it. Let your rule be to write not merely in such a way as to be understood, but rather so plainly that it will be impossible for any one of average intelligence to mis-understand you. Guthrie * tells us that an intelligent member of his first congregation at Arbirlot declined to take a second volume of Chalmers' works out of the library of the parish, on the ground that he had to look up for the meaning of so many of that author's words in the dictionary, and very often did not find them there, after all. Let not the lesson of such an incident be lost upon you. Choose the simplest and most familiar terms, and if at any time a word should recommend itself to you because of its novelty or its rarity, draw your pen through it, and put in its place the plainest substitute you can command. Never say " hebdomadal " when you mean " weekly,"† and do not lament that men have " perverse proclivities to prevarication," when you might express the same thought in Falstaff's words, " Lord, how this world is given to lying." Abjure all technical terms which, however familiar they may be to you, are utterly un-known to those who shall be your hearers. If you wish to remind men that conscience is God's voice within the soul, do not say, as I heard a young preacher say last year, that " conscience has its roots

---

* "Autobiography and Memoirs," Vol. I., p. 139.

† See further on this point, " The Preacher's Lantern," Vol. II., pp. 606–615.

in the soil of the absolute." All these modes of expression look very learned, but they are in reality only ridiculous. The end of communicating our thoughts to others is, that they may be moved thereby to purer and nobler lives; but, to secure that end, they must understand our words. And " I had rather speak five words with my understanding, that by my voice I might teach others also, than ten thousand words in an unknown tongue."*

Be not allured, either, by high-sounding adjectives. The business of an epithet is to give prominence to some quality the mention of which is needed to bring fully before the hearer's mind the matter of which we speak. But, as commonly employed by writers and preachers, adjectives are the merest expletives. They are inserted to ballast, or balance, the clauses of an antithesis, or to give padding to an ill-constructed sentence. They have an appearance of strength, but they are really the evidence of weakness. They are the inflated currency of rhetoric. Wealth of speech consists not in them, but in the ringing gold of thought. Use them only when there is something in the thought that corresponds to them; and when you come to ask yourselves concerning each, " Is this absolutely needful to express my meaning?" you will be surprised to discover how seldom they are required. In fact, it might be a good thing if one could have a waste-basket by his side, into which he could throw three out of every four epithets that rise to his pen. They

---

* 1 Corinthians xiv. 19.

give an exaggerated character to one's style, as if all the while he were straining on tip-toe or walking upon stilts. Nay, worse than all, they are many times *false,* and the employment of them is apt to foster an un-reality in our speech, which is akin to hypocrisy in conduct. There is an ethical element in composition as in other things, and Ruskin's canons in regard to architecture hold equally in the building of our ser-mons and other compositions. Let your style be true to your thought — that is, let it be a clear medium for the transmission of your thought—and then the individuality of your thinking will character-ize its expression also.

Take heed also of circumlocution. Go straight at your thought. When a man is in earnest, he will take the shortest way. Sometimes, indeed, it may be well to detain the mind of the auditor over your statement for a moment or two by judicious amplifi-cation, and so make sure that it is perfectly under-stood ; for, as Whately has said, bulk is necessary to digestion. Occasionally, too, one may indulge in that sort of reiteration for which Chalmers was remarkable, provided he can make it, as Chalmers did, the whirl-ings of the sling, which give swiftness to the stone that he is about to launch from it ; but, in general, the briefest and most direct expression we can give to our meaning is the best. Go forward steadily toward your goal, and keep just a little way ahead of your hearers. Do not gallop so quickly that they shall have difficulty in keeping up with you, and do not loiter so long over the flowers by the way-side or with the travelers whom you may chance to meet upon the road, that they shall be tempted to go on before you.

All this will require much study on your part, while yet you may get from the unthinking but little credit for your toil. That which by dint of patient effort you have made easy for others to comprehend, will not appear to them to be great. The clear is not often counted deep, and the "drumley" is very frequently reckoned profound. But then, that will be of no consequence to you if you be a true minister of Christ, for you have crucified self, and what is a reputation for learning or for depth to you if only you succeed in making plain to men the way of life, and persuading them to walk therein? Set to work, therefore, with your pen, and labor on, in season and out of season, that you may acquire the habit of giving simple, effective, and direct expression to the thoughts that arise within you.

Much I might say to you here from my own experience, for the pen has been almost constantly in my hand since I was thirteen years of age, but I prefer to bring before you the history of one of the ablest preachers of his country and his age. You have all heard of Thomas Binney, late minister of the King's Weigh-house Chapel, London,—that Archbishop of English Nonconformity, as one might call him—who so nobly moulded much of the Christian thought and legislation of his times. A few years before his death, in addressing the young men of his church, he gave them this interesting autobiographic sketch: "You

are all young men, engaged in business, but have to
improve your minds as best you can in your leisure
hours. Well, I was once in the same position. I was
seven years in a bookseller's concern, and during that
time my hours were, for two years, from seven A. M.
to eight P. M., and for five years from seven to seven;
under great pressure, I have sometimes been engaged
from six A. M. till ten P. M. But, somehow, all the
time, and especially from my fourteenth to my twen-
tieth year, I found opportunities for much reading
and a great deal of composition. I did not shirk,
however, my Latin and Greek, for I went for some
time two evenings in the week to an old Presbyterian
clergyman to learn the elements of the two languages,
and could read Cæsar and St. John. But my great
work was English. I read many of the best authors,
and I wrote largely both poetry and prose, and I did
so with much painstaking. I labored to acquire a
good style of expression as well as merely to express
my thoughts. Some of the plans I pursued were
rather odd, and produced odd results. I read the
whole of Johnson's 'Rambler,' put down all the new
words I met with—and they were a good many—
with their proper meanings, and then I wrote essays
in imitation of Johnson, and used them up. I did
the same with Thomson's 'Seasons,' and wrote blank
verse to use his words and also to acquire something
of music and rythm. And so I went on, sometimes
writing long poems in heroic verse; one on the 'Being of a God;' another, in two or three books, in blank
verse, in imitation of 'Paradise Lost.' I wrote essays

on the immortality of the soul; sermons; a tragedy, in three acts, and other things, very wonderful in their way, you may be sure. I think I can say I never fancied myself a poet or philosopher, but I wrote on and on to acquire the power to write with readiness; and I say to you, with a full conviction of the truth of what I say, that, having lived to gain some little reputation as a writer, I attribute all my success to what I did for myself, and to the habits I formed during those years to which I have thus referred."*

Few ministers had the power of Mr. Binney, whether in the preaching of sermons from a manuscript or in extempore delivery; and the foundation of much that he was and did was laid during these nights of work. But his experience is not by any means singular. Many of his brethren alike in England and America have, like him, "while their companions slept," been "toiling upwards in the night;" and something of the same self-discipline is essential to the success of any preacher. Go to work, then, young men, in a similar spirit, and very soon you will forget the labor in the delight which it will bring with it. Your interest will never flag; your enthusiasm will never tire. Ever new beauties will open up before you; ever new allurements will beckon you on; for in such pursuits you will find what Milton has called "the hill-side where is the right path of a virtuous and noble education, laborious, indeed, at its first

* "A Memorial of the late Rev. Thomas Binney, LL.D." Edited by John Stoughton, D.D., pp. 12, 13.

ascent, but else so smooth, so green, so full of goodly prospect and melodious sound on every side, that the harp of Orpheus was not more charming."†

All the things which as yet I have mentioned would be required, even if your business were to be the moving of men through the press. But your special work is to be that of preaching. You are to seek to sway your hearers by the living voice, and for this you have opportunities such as are accorded to no other profession. By common consent your people will give up a portion of every Lord's day for the very purpose of placing themselves under your guidance. They will come to the house of assembly with minds and hearts, in some measure, already prepared to listen to your words; but this, far from making you indifferent to the work of addressing them, will only spur you on to make the best of your opportunity. Accordingly, my treatment of the prerequisites to ministerial success would be signally incomplete, if I did not give prominence to the acquirement of *facility and distinctness in public speaking*. Without that, the arch which you build will lack the key-stone, which gives stability to all the rest. Without that, the arrow which you have constructed with such skill, and the bow which you have bent with such force, will be merely ornamental; it is effective utterance alone which can place the one upon the other, and give to the polished shaft the full momentum of the bow, so that it shall go whizzing to its mark.

† "Milton's Prose Works." Bohn's edition, Vol. III., p. 467.

I would not go so far as to say that articulate and earnest delivery is everything in a sermon; for truth is in words as well as in manner, and far more in the former than in the latter. Yet it is undeniable that effective utterance will give force even to a feeble sermon; while careless, hesitating, and indistinct speech, will make the finest composition fall flat and powerless upon the listeners' ears. In itself the manner may be far less important than the matter; but it is valuable, as giving its full force to the matter, and ought not to be lightly esteemed. You will do well, therefore, to cultivate elocution. But here, as in other things, you must be on your guard against artificiality. What you have to do is not to imitate another, but to cultivate yourselves. Do not covet "the stare and stark theatric practiced at the glass," but aim rather to cure yourselves of any awkwardnesses that may adhere to you, and to acquire any qualities in which you may be deficient. Do not make yourselves into lay-figures, which are the painter's poor substitutes for living men, but be yourselves, only yourselves, purged from your faults, and clothed with as much power as you can acquire by laborious exercise.

Seek first distinctness of articulation. Do not mistake loudness for clearness. No doubt a certain amount of volume is needed, if, as the phrase is, your voice would fill a large house. But hearers generally will tell you that they follow a speaker better when he is addressing them in moderate tones, than when, in impassioned mood, he is exerting his voice to the uttermost. The true secret here is to take sufficient time, and to give to every consonant its own proper sound. The vowels can take care of themselves. It is a mistake, therefore, to dwell, as some do, at inordinate length upon them. Such a habit always produces indistinctness. It is the province of the consonants to embank and confine the river of sound which a vowel makes, and if you do not keep them in good repair, the vowel will overflow so as to inundate the ear of the hearer, and make him unconscious of everything besides. They who are conversant with theatrical matters, tell us that by merely attending to this rule, an actor will make his slightest whisper audible to all in the building; and though our churches generally—the more's the pity—are not so well constructed for acoustical purposes as the theatres, yet by following this method, you may greatly increase your effectiveness, without making any larger expenditure of force.

Again, be not too rapid in your utterance. Do not put your hearers out of breath in their effort to keep up with you. This is the common vice of young orators. Therefore, be on your guard against it. Be not too slow either. But let your speed be regulated by the nature of that which at the moment you are saying. If you are laying down an important principle, then take time to give it weight; if you are prosecuting an intricate argument, then go forward leisurely, that your hearers may mark well every step. But if your are nearing your goal, and feel that you have thus far carried all before you, then give yourself full swing and rush on until you reach it.

Cultivate the art of appropriate emphasis. Do not let your sermons be like the letters of a school-miss, in which every other word is underscored. But study how to mark by the voice, the various points which need to be thereby denoted for the hearer's attention. Observe how in ordinary speech one unconsciously punctuates his sentences with emphasis, and seek to do the same in addressing your people. Above all, shun monotony as you would the plague. It is bad for the voice; it is bad, also, from its reflex influence on the composition of your sermons, for if you speak on a dead level, you will come at length to think on a dead level; and it is especially bad, from its soporific effect upon the audience. Rest your voice by varying skillfully its tones; give direct narrative in an easy and familiar style. Rise to a higher note when you become admonitory. Let pathos and solemnity be marked by the seriousness of your tone. Pause a moment and change your key when you wish to introduce an illustration; and as you pass from one division of your subject to another, give your hearers time to gather themselves up again before you make a new demand upon their attention.

For this purpose you will need thorough self-possession; and nothing but practice will give you that. Have yourself well in hand, so that you can always command your powers; and beware of letting your-self be carried away, up into some shrieking falsetto, by which for the whole remainder of your discourse your voice will be destroyed.

It is easier to give you these counsels than it is to

follow them. But drill and culture will do much. Read frequently aloud. Embrace every opportunity that offers, whether in the debating society, or elsewhere, for the practice of speaking. Be your own most remorseless critic ; and lay well to heart the admonitions of any friend whose love to you permits you to see yourself through the eyes of one who is deeply interested in your welfare. Be not discouraged though the work be arduous, for so long as the story of Demosthenes and the pebbles shall be told, no one needs despair. His perseverance in these details, indeed, did not make him an orator, but it did enable him to overcome defects of utterance, which would have made all his other powers comparatively worthless, so far as eloquence was concerned. You may not attain his greatness, but, by perseverance, his example warrants you to hope that you may acquire distinctness and energy of speech.

I have dwelt so long on these points, that I have left myself but little space to speak of one prerequisite to pulpit efficiency, which is as important as the others, but which now I can do little more than name. I mean that quality which we call *common sense*. Alas! how many preachers otherwise admirably equipped have failed for lack of that! And yet it is difficult to give a definition of it. We may describe it as an intuitive perception of the fitness of things, so that he who is endowed with it will always do that which is appropriate to the circumstances. It is different from caution, or what is generally known as prudence; inasmuch as that is the result of calculation, while common sense is rather an immediate perception. It keeps a man from making, as people say, a fool of himself, either by stupid speech in the pulpit, or by ridiculous conduct out of it. The breach of it may not be precisely an immorality, but it is an indecorum, the commission of which stamps him at once as an ass. He who lacks this quality has no right to be a minister, for he turns the most sacred things into a laughing-stock, and makes a burlesque of the office itself.

Nor can this defect be easily supplied. The story goes that when a Scottish farmer went to his pastor to consult him as to sending his son to college with a view to his becoming a minister, the good man sought to dissuade him from his purpose, and on being asked for the reason, said, " I tell you, man, he wants common sense. Now, if a man want wealth he may get that ; if he want learning, he may get that ; if he want the grace of God, he may get that ; but if he want common sense, he'll never get that." This witness is true ; albeit, the youth concerning whom these words were said, was very far indeed from having no common sense, for he was none other than George Lawson, who afterwards became distinguished as a professor of theology, and was known over all the country as a Christian Socrates. Still, it is true, that common sense cannot be acquired. Yet in those who have it, it may be cultivated and increased ; and presuming that you already possess it, let me urge you to give good heed to its suggestions.

Do not set yourselves to shock the feelings of
your hearers by your wanton defiance of all their
prepossessions, or if you will, their prejudices.
Become all things to all men, that you may by
all means save some. A mountebank may be in
his place in the ring of the circus, but he has no business in the pulpit; and all the learning he may possess, or all the eloquence he may display, will not
make amends for the lack of propriety which he
evinces. I know that some will be ready to fling at
me the quotation about being "content to dwell in
decencies forever." But I protest that it is not needful to be dull in order to be decent; and I altogether
deny that in order to do men good, one must put on
the cap, and ring the bells of the fool. "It is pitiful
to court a grin, when we should woo a soul;" and,
however much one may enjoy the witicisms of the
clown in other places, common sense says that the
preacher, with the Word of God before him, and immortal souls seeking life and comfort at his lips, should
be at least serious.

But I may not conclude without reminding you,
that even these prerequisites which I have enumera-
ted, will not make a preacher. I do not believe that
any one can rise to the highest efficiency in the pulpit
without them, but still alone they will not suffice.
They must be all vitalized and concentrated on one object by the consecration of the man to the service of
Christ, and of his fellow-men in the work of the ministry. They are the separate strands, but they must

be spun together into one by the intense love which the preacher has, on the one hand for the Lord Jesus Christ, and on the other for human souls. Thus " the cords of a man," manifold though they be, become unified into " the bond of love " wherewith the hearers are to be drawn to God. Let this never be forgotten by us, for it is this only that can bring our natural talents or acquired abilities to bear upon our work. Still, the question addressed to him who would become a preacher, is that which was three times pressed upon the humble Peter, " Lovest thou me ?" not, observe, Lovest thou the work? but, " Lovest thou *me ?*" and when we can answer, " Thou knowest all things, Thou knowest that I love Thee," we have at once the commission and the qualification to feed the sheep and the lambs of the flock, for that love will consecrate the whole man, and make him all magnetic.

LECTURE IV.

THE THEME AND RANGE OF THE PULPIT.

LECTURE IV.

THE THEME AND RANGE OF THE PULPIT.

THE special work which as ministers we have to do, is the preaching of the Gospel. We have been "allowed of God," like Paul, "to be put in trust with the Gospel;"* and to us also, is committed "the ministry of reconciliation; to wit, that God was in Christ, reconciling the world unto himself, not imputing their trespasses unto them."† It is of the highest importance, therefore, that we should rightly understand the theme which we have to treat, and the range which it commands.

The Gospel is a message of good news. It takes for granted that men are sinners, under sentence, and carrying in themselves a nature that is prone to evil, and averse to good; and it brings to them an assurance that they may be forgiven and renewed, through faith in Jesus Christ. Thus the Lord himself said to Nicodemus, "As Moses lifted up the serpent in the wilderness, even so must the Son of man be lifted up, that whosoever believeth in Him should not perish, but have eternal life. For God so loved the world that He gave His only begotten Son, that whosoever

---

* 1 Thessalonians ii. 4.   † 2 Corinthians v. 19.

believeth in Him should not perish, but have ever-
lasting life."*   And again in connection with the introduction to Him of the Greeks at Jerusalem, He
said, "And I, if I be lifted up from the earth, will
draw all men unto me."†

Similarly, Paul defines the Gospel to be the setting
forth of Christ Jesus by God, "to be a propitiation
through faith in His blood, to declare His righteousness for the remission of sins that are past, through
the forbearance of God, to declare at this time His
righteousness, that He might be just, and the justifier
of him that believeth."‡   So also, in describing the
substance of his preaching to the Corinthians he says:
"I delivered unto you, first of all, that which I also
received, how that Christ died for our sins, according
to the Scriptures, and that He was buried, and
that He rose again the third day, according to the
Scriptures."§   And if one should ask what he means
by the phrase, "Christ died for our sins," he is answered by this declaration made elsewhere, "God
hath made Him to be sin for us, who knew no sin ;
that we might be made the righteousness of God in
Him."‖   So important did the great apostle deem this
truth, that he says to the Corinthians, "We preach
Christ crucified ;"¶ and affirms that when he went to
them at first, "he determined not to know anything
among them, save Jesus Christ, and Him crucified."**

---

* John iii. 14–16.   † John xii. 32.
‡ Romans iii. 25–26.   § 1 Corinthians xv. 3–5.
‖ 2 Corinthians v. 21.   ¶ 1 Corinthians i. 23.
** 1 Corinthians ii. 2.

While to the Galatians he says, "God forbid that I should glory, save in the cross of our Lord Jesus Christ, by whom the world is crucified unto me, and I unto the world."*

Many more passages might be quoted to the like effect, all going to show that the central interest of the Gospel is in a person, namely, *Jesus Christ;* in a certain fact about that person, namely, that *He was crucified;* and in the relation of that fact on the one hand to God, and on the other hand to men, so that human sinners believing in Jesus, may be righteously forgiven, and renewed in the spirit of their minds.

This, then, is the message with which we are entrusted, and which it is alike our privilege and our duty to proclaim to men. But if we have rightly described it, then it must be evident at a glance, that if we would proclaim it intelligibly, we must have much to say both about the nature of Christ's person, and the character of His death. To call upon men constantly to "come to Christ," or to repeat perpetually the words of Paul to the jailer, "Believe on the Lord Jesus Christ," without at the same time telling them who Jesus is, and what it is to come to Him, and believe on Him, is the merest mockery. It is using the name of Christ as if it were some cabalistic charm, and reducing the Gospel message to a mere empty formula. If, therefore, we would be effective preachers, we must be ready to give an answer to him that asks us, "Who is Jesus, that I may believe on Him? and what was there in His dying that has any relation to me?"

But the attempt to answer these questions, will bring

* Galatians vi. 14.

us at once into the region of doctrine, and there we are met with the popular cry, " Preach Christ, and leave doctrines alone." But how is it possible to do anything of the kind ? The word Christ is not a mere abstraction. It is the name of a person, and if we attempt to tell who or what He is, we are giving forth a doctrine about His person. Equally if we endeavor to describe what the significance of His death is, we are putting forth a doctrine of the atonement. Thus, not only those of us who are styled evangelical are guilty of doctrinal preaching. If we shall say that Jesus Christ was only a man, that is a doctrine of His person, as really as is the assertion that in Him the eternal Word was made flesh. If we shall affirm, that His death was nothing more than that of a martyr, that is a doctrine about Christ's crucifixion, as really as is the declaration that He died the just in the stead of the unjust. If, again, we should try to explain what it is to come to Jesus or to believe on Him, the effort, if successful, will issue in a doctrinal sermon on the nature of faith.

In truth, gentlemen, there is nothing more absurd than this clamor against doctrine, for they who raise it do not seem to see that there is beneath the cry itself a doctrine, to the effect that it makes no matter what a man believes, if he only say that he is resting upon Christ. But the Christ that saves, is the Christ that is revealed in the Gospels, not the mere idea of Him which a man may form in his own mind. It is not believing on Christ as I have shaped Him for myself, but rather believing on the Christ that is set before me in the Gospel, that saves me; and so it is of immense consequence that I should have a right view both of His person and work. If, therefore, you mean to be successful preachers, you will do well to shut your ears to all that senseless outcry against doctrine which has become a part of the most fashionable cant of the day. One of the most eloquent of living English nonconformists, has said very truly here: " It is impossible to preach Christ without preaching dogma, unless I confine myself to a bare recital of the mere externals of the history: and if I could do that, it were no Gospel. For what of good news is there in the dry chronicle that He lived and died, any more than in the same bald record about any other man? Is the mere story of His death a gospel? Does it not need a commentary explanatory of the fact to make it that? The history becomes a gospel by the presence of the doctrine as touching His person, that He is the Son of God: as touching His death, that it is the sacrifice for the sins of the world. Without so much of dogma, the facts are not seen; without so much they are powerless to bless; and our Gospel is of another sort, or rather it is not one at all, unless we too can declare this as 'the gospel which we preached, how that Christ'—the very name being the condensation of a whole system of doctrines—'died for our sins according to the Scriptures.'"*

---

* " The Gospel for the Day," being the President's address before the annual meeting of the Baptist Union of Great Britain and Ireland, by Rev. Alexander Maclaren, Manchester. Reported *verbatim* in " The Baptist," April 30, 1875. One of the noblest discourses of a very noble man.

Unless, therefore, you are prepared to say something very definite, both concerning the nature of Christ's person, and concerning the character and efficacy of His death, you had better never enter the pulpit. The notion of many seems to be that vagueness is the prime excellence in a sermon. They are always dealing in the indefinite. You cannot make out from their words what, according to their view, Christ is, whether incarnate God, or simply the highest style of man ; and though they can speak of the "cross of Christ," and of "Christ crucified," you cannot but feel that the words to them are mere empty symbols. Now, all such preaching is a waste of words. Gentlemen, it is the positive element in your teaching that will, through God's spirit, be powerful with your hearers ; and if you cannot give any distinct utterance as to who Christ is, or what He has done, then all your criticisms of the ordinary evangelical doctrines will be valueless to the anxious inquirer, and may be even injurious in unsettling the mind of some one who has been but slenderly ballasted with biblical knowledge.

Preach doctrine, therefore. Do not proclaim it as if it were the Saviour, but let your doctrine define the Saviour to the minds of those who wait upon your ministry. Do not make your treatment of doctrine an occasion for metaphysical display, but seek rather by your dogmatic teachings to give clearness and force to the apprehension which your hearers have of truth. Above all, seek to have your doctrines vitalized by their connection with Christ, so

that they may appear either to flow from Him, or to lead
up to Him, and then they will give to your discourses
a symmetry and a strength which otherwise they
could not possess; and save them from degenerating
into soft, molluscous, and plastic things, which may
be squeezed by the hearer into any shape, or turned
by him into any direction. "He who teaches," says
Bautain, "has always a doctrine to expound."* It is
impossible to give a pupil any correct idea either of
philosophy or of any one of the natural sciences, unless
there be connected with the facts which are set before his mind, a commentary of doctrine. The name
of Kepler is a name and nothing more, until we have
associated it with those laws, that is doctrines, of motion of which he was the earliest exponent; and the
place of Newton in the history of science cannot be
described by us, unless we give an exposition of that
doctrine of gravitation which was his generalization
from the facts of nature. Nay more, we cannot enforce the plainest moral precept without finding ourselves ultimately in the region of doctrine; for if we
urge upon a man the duty of honesty, and he should
ask us on what ground we do so, then, whether we reply, "because honesty is the best policy," or "because
honesty is commanded by God," or "because honesty
is required by the greatest good of the greatest number," our answer is a doctrine. Every practical
precept must stand thus upon some doctrine; and so
we are forced to conclude that this modern antipathy

* "The Art of Extempore Speaking," by M. Bautain. Scrib-
ner's edition, p. 141.

to doctrine is not so much an opposition to doctrine in itself, as to those doctrines which evangelical preachers love to set forth. And in that aspect of it, the prejudice is not so modern after all, for it had an existence even in the days of Paul, whose doctrine of Christ crucified was to the Jews a " stumbling-block," and to the Greeks " foolishness."

In spite, therefore, of all that is said by the superficial to the contrary, let your preaching to sinners be an exposition to them of the doctrine of the cross. Be not content merely with the presentation to them of the incarnation. Paul did not say, " I determined not to know anything among you but Jesus Christ," and then stop there! He added with special emphasis, " and *Him* crucified," for in the union of the two, and the blessing which flowed therefrom, the Gospel in his view consisted. Even if we accept the incarnation as a fact, the Lord Jesus could have had no saving relationship to us, if He had not died for our sins ; while again, His death could have had no value as an atonement for sin, if He had not been incarnate God. It is not simply that one died for us, but it is that He who so died was such an one as the Son of God. This is the essence of the atonement, which " declared God's righteousness," even in the forgiveness of a believing sinner. Here is mercy righteously manifested to the guilty.

Wherever else you look, in air, on earth, or in the sea, there is law—hard, remorseless law—good as long as you obey it, but relentless the moment you run counter to its requirements. Combustion has no mercy if you thrust your finger into the flames; gravitation has no consideration for the consequences on you if you step over a precipice; the sea knows no compassion if you fall into its depths. Nowhere in nature can you discern anything of mercy to the law-breaker. Its aspect is, in this regard, very terrible.

But in the cross of Christ there is a provision made for showing mercy to the sinner; while yet the law which the sinner has broken is honored and "established."* There is love in it that "passeth knowledge." And we must take heed so to preach it, that men shall recognize that it flowed from the heart of God as He yearned for their deliverance from the consequences of their sins. The death of Christ did not purchase God's love for the world; but it opened up a way in which that love could be righteously exercised in the forgiving of sin. Thus these two principles, love and righteousness, are the two great elements of the power of the cross. The love fills and melts the sinner's heart; and the righteousness satisfies his conscience, so that as soon as he believes the truth which is in Jesus Christ and Him crucified, he is filled with a joy which is unspeakable, and a peace which is perennial.

That very faculty within him which before upbraided him with his guilt, now rests satisfied in the assurance of a pardon which is sealed by righteousness. Without that seal, however, he could have no abiding comfort, and so, even if the atonement had not been

---

* Romans iii. 31.

needed to meet the demands of the divine law, it would be required to satisfy the conscience of the sinner himself. He cannot have permanent peace in a pardon that ignores justice. But because through the cross the love and righteousness of God are seen harmoniously working out his forgiveness, he is at rest.

Let us take care lest in our preaching we " put asunder " those two things which in the Gospel God has so thoroughly " joined together." We must not exalt the love without making mention of the righteousness. Indeed, if there were no righteousness, making the death imperative in order to the salvation of men, it is hard to see how there could be love in the dying. But neither, on the other hand, must we exalt the righteousness in such a way as to obscure the love. In the one case the Gospel will be made to wear an aspect of indifference to evil, and the hearer may fall into the terrible mistake of supposing that the more he sins, the more the grace of God will abound toward him. In the other it will be made to assume an appearance of terror, which will make men " exceedingly fear and quake," like the Israelites at the base of Sinai. But when we give each element its proper prominence, the love attracts to God, and the righteousness restrains from sin. The man of science takes a piece of limestone, and bringing two different kinds of gases to bear upon it, he makes it glow with a brightness that turns night well-nigh into day. Something like that, only in a spiritual way, is wrought on the stony heart of the sinner when he understands and believes what the cross of Christ proclaims to him, for as the love and righteousness which it reveals come streaming in upon him, they dispel the darkness of his misery, and irradiate him with the light of heaven's own joy.

This was the Gospel which, as proclaimed by Paul, was demonstrated to be the power of God unto salvation. This was the Gospel which, as preached by Luther, roused Europe from the slumber of centuries and shook popery to its centre. And if we to-day would re-clothe it with its ancient might, we must hold and teach it as Paul did. They tell us, indeed, that we must adapt our sermons to the necessities of our age; but, while in some minor respects the advice is good, we must beware of supposing that we are either to add to, or take from, those essential elements in which the Gospel, as revealed in the New Testament, consists. The preaching most adapted to any age is *the preaching of the Gospel*, not in dry, dogmatic formulæ, nor in fierce and controversial spirit, but in the way of simple and positive statement. Let us tell men that " Christ Jesus came into the world to save sinners ; " let us commend to them the love of God " in that while we were yet sinners, Christ died for us." Let us teach that they are to be saved, not by sacramental efficacy, or ritual observances, or even moral worth, but simply and alone through faith in Him who loved them and gave Himself for them. That is the Gospel which every age needs, and its adaptation to the human heart is made gloriously apparent wherever it is earnestly proclaimed.

We may learn much here from the example of Paul on his visit to Corinth. There he found two classes of minds, the representatives of two opposite tendencies. The one sought a philosophy, and the other a sign. Yet Paul preached to both "Jesus Christ and Him crucified." That which they did not wish, was yet that which they most needed. And so to-day; in the face of rationalism and ritualism, whose supporters are the legitimate successors of the Greek and the Jew in apostolic times, we shall find that all our power in the pulpit will lie, not in fierce controversy, nor in trimming concession, but in the plain, earnest enforcement of the good old truth that "Jesus Christ died for our sins according to the Scriptures, and that he was buried, and that he rose again the third day according to the Scriptures." As Mr. Maclaren has said, in the address from which I have already quoted, "There is as true adaptation in rowing against or athwart the stream as in going with it; and unless this age has got rid of the one-sidedness which has always hitherto affected the current beliefs of a period, perhaps the truest adaptation of a message to its wants, is to bring into prominence what it overlooks, and to emphasize the proclamation of what it does *not* believe."* Preach the Gospel as Paul preached it, and you may look for a success similar to that which crowned his labors.

Just as I was entering on my ministry at Liverpool, I fell in with a copy of Spenser's "Pastoral Sketches,"

---

* Maclaren's Address at the Annual Meeting of the Baptist Union, as before.

with an Introductory Essay on the Preaching of the Gospel, by the late Mr. James, of Birmingham. I was in a mood to be impressed, and a severe domestic affliction through which I was then passing made me more susceptible than even the beginning of a new pastorate would of itself have rendered me. So I was profoundly moved by Mr. James's arguments and appeals. I have since read them, again and again, and have seen little remarkable about them; but, as perused then, they led me to set my whole ministry to the key of the cross. I tried simply, faithfully, and affectionately to tell "the old, old story of Jesus and His love." Very soon inquirers came to talk with me. I was cheered and encouraged by receiving new converts at every communion. This kept me from ever yielding to the temptation to turn aside from the great central themes, and my success, such as it was, in that sphere, was owing, I am thoroughly persuaded, to the fact that I tried always to keep the cross in sight, and sought always to hide myself behind my Lord.

When, again, I was crossing the Atlantic to take charge of my present congregation, not one of whom I had ever seen, I found the "Life of Chalmers" in the library of the ship, and amid the anxiety and suspense of my heart, as I felt that I had not "passed this way heretofore," I was greatly cheered and encouraged by the account of the effects produced by the preaching of that great man in his later life at Kilmany, and in his glorious ministry at Glasgow. This led me to resolve anew that in the ministry of the Broadway Tabernacle, I would, as in Liverpool, seek to preach so that my hearers "should see no man save Jesus only," and if I have had any measure of success, this is the secret of it all. I feel almost as if it were an impertinence to speak thus. Why should I presume, as it were, to endorse the Gospel thus? and yet, as an elder brother, I may surely tell you of my limited experience, in the hope that in after years you will have to say to me, "Now, we believe it, not for thy saying," but because we have tried it ourselves, and we know that it is "the power of God unto salvation to every one that believeth."

But the minister of the Gospel in these days is a pastor as well as a preacher, and so he has to do with those who are already Christians, as well as with those who are "ignorant and out of the way." It will be his business not merely to stand at the "wicket-gate" and help men through that as they set out on their pilgrimage to the "celestial city;" but also to make up to them afterwards at their several stages on their journey, and to give them such assistance and direction as they need. The "Evangelist" who goes from place to place may content himself with performing the office of John the Baptist, esteeming his joy fulfilled when he has introduced the sinner to his Saviour. But the Christian pastor has to "go before his flock," and "lead them out" and "find pasture" for them appropriate to their nourishment. He has to watch over and encourage the development of character in the Christian, as well as to call on the sinner to " repent and be converted ; " and while, of course, he will greatly rejoice over the conversion of sinners, he will rejoice no less over the growth in grace of those who are already in Christ. He must be on his guard against devoting himself to either of these departments of his work to the exclusion of the other, for only in the proper prosecution of them both, the symmetry and completeness of his ministry will be secured.

Judging from my own experience, you will be most apt to set yourselves in the beginning of your career, to secure the conversion of sinners ; while, perhaps, as you advance in the work, you may be tempted to run into the other extreme, and preach only to those who are already in the Church. But in neither case will there be a " right division " of the word of truth ; and your aim ought to be, on every occasion, to give to each " his portion in season."

Still, as there is a tendency in these days among many to restrict the ministry to one phase of truth merely, I may be forgiven if I dwell for a moment or two on the importance of seeking in your discourses the spiritual profit of that large class of your hearers who have made an open confession of their faith in Christ, and who are needing either to be warned against dangers which threaten to impair their strength, or to be encouraged under trials that are pressing heavily upon their hearts. It has come to be taken for granted in many quarters, that the success of a ministry is to be gauged simply by the number of conversions which have occurred in its course ; and this has led too many churches to bend all their energies toward the securing of such accessions to their membership, as if that were the sole end to be attained. Pastor, Sabbath-school teachers, office-bearers, members, labor and pray in public, and exhort in private, in order that they may lead men to Christ, and to a public confession of Him, and then, when they have got their names on the communion roll, they leave them to take care of themselves, and they go and look after others. But, in reality, this is only the beginning with them, and to leave them thus untended is the greatest possible mistake.

We cry out against the heedlessness of those parents who so neglect their offspring as to leave them an easy prey to the diseases which make such havoc on little children. But "*infant mortality*" is by no means unknown in our churches, any more than in our cities, and I fear that the disappearance of many who were once written down as "hopefully converted" is due to the fact that so many of our ministers and their coadjutors never concern themselves with any other topic than conversion. Now that is unquestionably a most important theme, and the direction of inquirers is an interesting and intensely exciting department of ministerial labor; but it is not the whole work of the pastor. "Doth the ploughman plough all day to sow? doth he open and break the clods of his ground? When he hath made plain the face thereof, doth he not cast abroad the fitches, and scatter the cummin, and cast in the principal wheat and the appointed barley and the rye in

their place? For his God doth instruct him to discretion, and doth teach him."* Something more than
ploughing is required for successful husbandry; and
more is needed in the culture of a parish than the
preaching of conversion, or the saying to men, " Believe on the Lord Jesus Christ, and ye shall be saved."
Faith is good; is, indeed, indispensable, but it is
only the first round of the ladder, and we ought not
to be content until our hearers have added to it,
courage, and knowledge, and temperance, and patience, and godliness, and brotherly kindness, and
love, for in that way alone can they " make their
calling and election sure."

Thus in our ministry we have not simply to make
known to men the way of salvation, as Peter did on
the day of Pentecost, and in the house of Cornelius,
and as Paul did to the jailer, and to his hearers in Thes-
salonica and Berea, but we have also to do a work
not unlike that which these apostles performed in the
Epistles which came afterwards from their pens. Or
as Paul has said to Timothy, we have to "reprove,
rebuke, and exhort with all long-suffering and doctrine."† We are to expose prevailing sins, warn against
existing temptations, incite to higher holiness, and
stimulate to the performance of "works of faith and
labors of love."

Yet, not unfrequently, when a sermon has been
preached exposing some social evil, and unfolding
the remedy by which alone it can be removed, the

---

* Isaiah xxviii. 24–26. † 2 Tim. iv. 2.

minister will be told that he is going aside from his proper work as an ambassador for Christ, and some earnest but narrow soul may say to him, "Preach the Gospel, and leave these subjects alone; remember him who said, 'I determined not to know anything among you save Jesus Christ and Him crucified.'"

Now, as is abundantly evident from what I have already said, I find no fault with the sentiment of these words. Nay, rather when rightly understood, they strike the key-note of every evangelical ministry; but my complaint is, that those who quote them for our benefit, seem to have no correct idea of the meaning which Paul himself attached to them. He did not intend to say that every time he opened his lips, he would tell over again the story of the Cross, but rather that as the means of saving men from their sins, he would set nothing else before them than Jesus Christ and Him crucified; and further, that the Cross was to be the great centre of his teaching, from which he claimed and exercised the liberty of treating every subject in the whole circumference of human duty and experience.

I wonder what those who would restrict us to the simple invitation of sinners to come to Christ, as if that alone were evangelical preaching, would say to the Apostle James, if he were to occupy a modern pulpit and give his epistle as a sermon. Nay, I wonder what they make of the very Epistle of Paul, from which their quotation is taken, for within the short compass of its sixteen chapters he discusses such questions as the propriety of marriage in a time of peril, the eating of meat offered to idols, the going to law before heathen tribunals, the right manner of conducting public worship, the evil of ecclesiastical divisions, and even so commonplace a matter as a benevolent collection. Were Paul and James unevangelical? No; they were in all this most truly preaching the Gospel, because they were bringing the principles which underlie its message, to bear upon the circumstances and conduct of those whom they addressed.

The truth is, that the Gospel is related to everything which affects the happiness and the holiness of men; and its minister not only may, but ought to show its relations to these things in his discourses. Only let him see to it that when he is seeking to elevate men, he uses the Cross as his lever, and then while his discourses are helpful to believers, they will at the same time be the means of awakening and converting sinners. There is a way of getting at the hearts and consciences of the unconverted, even when we are furnishing guidance and encouragement to the true Christian; and on the other hand, we may deal with sinners in such a way as shall also stimulate and quicken saints.

Indeed, if we care to study true wisdom here, we shall aim at having in every sermon a word for every hearer; and if you ask me how that is to be attained, I will set you to the study of those Epistles to which I have already so frequently referred. Whatever may be the immediate object which Paul is seeking, he tries to attain that object by the Cross.

Thus, in reproving the unseemly divisions that had sprung up in the Corinthian Church, he says: "Is Christ divided? was Paul crucified for you, or were you baptized in the name of Paul?"* Now, weighty as that was as an argument for union and brotherly-love, it has in it, also, an incidental preaching of the Gospel so simple, yet so full, that some poor sinner might have caught at it with joy.

Again, in enforcing the duty of maintaining purity of discipline in the Church, he uses this plea: "Purge out, therefore, the old leaven, that ye may be a new lump as ye are unleavened. For even Christ our passover is sacrificed for us; therefore, let us keep the feast, not with old leaven, neither with the leaven of malice and wickedness, but with the unleavened bread of sincerity and truth." † Now, there is a whole syllogism wrapped up in the illustration that is here employed; but what I wish you particularly to observe is, that the centre of the illustration itself, is a decla-ration of the Gospel. So that while aiming after the purifying of the Church, he does at the same time clearly and simply unfold the great truth that Christ is sacrificed for us.

In a similar manner, while denouncing the sin of fornication, he puts the matter thus: "What? know ye not that your body is the temple of the Holy Ghost which is in you, which ye have of God, and ye are not your own? for ye are bought with a price: therefore, glorify God in your body and in your spirit, which are God's." ‡ Here again, you observe, while exposing sin, he does it in such a way as at the same time to preach "Christ crucified." They say that when one of the most interesting ruins in the city

---

* 1 Corinthians i. 13.   † 1 Corinthians v. 7, 8.
‡ 1 Corinthians vi. 19, 20.

of Rome was in danger of destruction, because the neighboring inhabitants were continually removing stones from it for their own buildings, the reigning Pontiff put a stop to the vandalism of the people, by consecrating the venerable remains and setting up the Cross in the midst of them. Now, similarly here, Paul has put the Cross in the centre of human life, and so has made it sacrilege for the believer to take any portion of his being, or any fraction of his time and give it to another than his Lord. But he could not put the Cross there without letting it be seen, and so here again, he has preached the Gospel most effectively, even when he was seeking specially to warn his readers against a particular sin.

But to mention only one more instance; when he is pleading the cause of the poor saints at Jerusalem, he is careful so to do it, as at the same time to give a very striking and comprehensive summary of the Gospel. Thus he writes: " For ye know the grace of our Lord Jesus Christ, that though He was rich, yet for your sakes He became poor, that ye through His poverty might be rich." * It is singular that such an expression—so beautiful, so suggestive, and every way so worthy of the sacrifice it describes—should have come thus incidentally from the pen of the Apostle. He was presenting a motive to the Corinthians to induce them to give a good collection, and lo! at the same time, he preaches the Gospel in language which is, even with him, unusual in its energy and elevation.

---

* 2 Corinthians viii. 9.

Now, all this shows us what Paul meant by preaching "Christ and Him crucified;" and lets us see how,
even when we are dealing with those "called to be
saints," we may have also words "in season" for the
sinner. For the Epistles to the Corinthians are not
singular in the characteristic which I have endeavored
to point out to you. The other letters of Paul, and
those of his fellow-apostles, John, Peter, and James,
are equally remarkable in this respect; and if, with
the instances which I have particularized, in mind,
you study these productions, you will see that evangelical preaching is something far more important
than the mere iteration to men of the Gospel invitation to "come to Jesus."

The Gospel, as Paul preached it, was far-reaching
enough in its application to touch at every point the
conduct and experiences of men. The Cross, as he
used it, was an instrument of the widest range and
of the greatest power. When, therefore, I insist that
you like him should "preach Jesus Christ and Him
crucified," I do not mean to make the pulpit for you
a battery, of such a nature that the guns upon it can
strike only such vessels as happen to pass immediately
in front of its embrasures. On the contrary, I turn it for
you into a tower, whereon is mounted a swivel-cannon,
which can sweep the whole horizon of human life,
and strike down all immorality, and ungodliness, and
selfishness, and sin. I do not shut you into a small
chamber having but one outlook, and even that into
a narrow court; but I place you in an observatory
with a revolving telescope that can command the
landscape round and round, and sweep, besides, the

hemisphere of the stars. I do not mean that you should keep continually repeating the words of "the faithful saying" like a parrot-cry, until every particle of meaning has dropped out of them; but rather, that you should make application of the great principles that lie beneath the Cross, to the ever-varying circumstances and occurrences of life, and that in such a way as at once to succor the Christian and arrest and convert the sinner. I do not mean that you should disdain the aids of literature, or refuse to use such illustrations as science may supply; but rather that, while employing all these, you should make them always subservient to this central theme, and ever turn their light upon the Master's face. I do not mean that you should decline to venture with your hearers for a voyage over the ocean of truth; but rather that while sailing forth, you should be careful still to have your first parallel of longitude passing through Calvary, that so you may judge of all things else by their relation to the Cross, and that, ever as you have opportunity, you should beseech sinners to be reconciled to God.

Is there anywhere, gentlemen, a finer field for usefulness than the pulpit is when thus employed? Is there anywhere a more powerful instrument for good than the Cross of Christ when thus applied? Go forth determined to use them both to the full, after the pattern of the great Apostle; and though you may not have at any time such seasons of excitement as men commonly call revivals, your ministry will be a constant revival, for you will be always gladdened by the occurrence of conversions, while at the same

time you are encouraged by beholding your children
" walking in the truth."

He will never find the pulpit either a narrow place
or a useless place, who enters it in the spirit in which
the Lord Himself began His ministry, and feels that
ne, too, can say, at least with some measure of truth,
" The Spirit of the Lord God is upon me ; because
the Lord hath anointed me to preach good tidings
unto the meek; He hath sent me to bind up the
broken-hearted, to proclaim liberty to the captives,
and the opening of the prison to them that are bound ;
to proclaim the acceptable year of the Lord, and the
day of vengeance of our God; to comfort all that
mourn ; to appoint unto them that mourn in Zion, to
give unto them beauty for ashes, the oil of joy for
mourning, the garment of praise for the spirit of
heaviness, that they might be called trees of righteousness, the planting of the Lord, that He might
be glorified." *   Go, gentlemen, and do that work,
using the Cross of Christ as your great instrument,
and you will find a sphere ample enough for all your
energies, and success large enough to fill your hearts
with joy.

---

* Isaiah lxi. 1–3.   I cannot quote this passage without directing attention to the volume written in exposition of it, by my old
friend and neighbor, the Rev. Alexander Macleod, D.D., Birken-
head, England.   His work on these verses, entitled " Christus
Consolator," is a most valuable treatise, vindicating successfully
the liberty of the pulpit to deal with social questions, and furnishing an excellent example of the best way of handling very delicate subjects.

LECTURE V.

THE QUALITIES OF EFFECTIVE PREACHING—IN THE
SERMON.

LECTURE V.

THE QUALITIES OF EFFECTIVE PREACHING—IN THE SERMON.

THAT is effective preaching which convinces the intellect, stirs the heart, and quickens the conscience of the hearer, so that he is moved to believe the truth which has been presented to him, or to take the course which has been enforced upon him.

This result cannot be produced, in any case, without the agency of the Holy Ghost; yet it is never to be forgotten that, in bringing it about, that Divine person works by means, which have, even in themselves, a fitness to secure the end in view. Now of these means, so far as they are connected with the Christian ministry, the sermon is the most important; and the preacher ought always to seek that his discourse shall have in it special adaptation to effect the result which, at the moment, he has set before him.

There is no inconsistency between his faith in the necessity of the agency of the Spirit, and his exertion to have his sermon such as shall be signally fitted to impress his hearers; nay, rather the more intelligently be believes that he is a "laborer together with God," the more diligently will he work to make his discourse as excellent as possible. The husbandman knows that he cannot make the seed grow; yet while he looks to

God for the increase, he is himself careful to treat each sort of soil as its nature requires, and to give to each kind of crop the peculiar attention that its character demands. And in like manner, though the preacher is aware that God alone can make his sermon effectual in the spiritual profiting of his hearers, yet "because he is wise," he seeks "to find out acceptable words" which shall be "as goads, and as nails fastened by the masters of assemblies." *

There are, indeed, extremists who affirm that all attention paid by the preacher to the preparation of his discourse, is just so much dishonor done to the Holy Spirit; but such an opinion is utterly opposed to the fundamental principle of the ministry of the Gospel. The peculiar glory of that service is, that it is a sacrifice. The preacher lays both himself and his sermon upon the altar, that his Lord may use them for the highest and holiest purposes. Now, every sacrifice should be the very noblest we can offer. Hence, just because the minister feels that he is consecrated (not by any formal ordination, but by his own voluntary dedication and by the anointing of the Holy Ghost) to Christ, he seeks to make himself "thoroughly furnished" for his work; and because he makes his sermon an offering to Christ, he labors to have it the best he can produce. Out of the very love of his heart he endeavors to make his discourse the very finest tribute which he can lay at his Master's feet, for

> "Love still delights to bring her best,
> And where love is, her offering evermore is blest."

---

* Ecclesiastes xii. 10, 11.

When, therefore, he is acting on this principle, he is not to be told that he is dishonoring the Spirit. It seems very pious to be thus jealous for the honor of the Holy Ghost, but it is in reality very impious, and the minister who seeks to glorify God by systematically neglecting the preparation of his discourses, will find in the end that he has only covered himself with disgrace. In the work of " winning souls," as in other departments of human activity, it is " the hand of the diligent " that " maketh rich."

There is, therefore, no reason, so far as the prerogative of the Holy Ghost is concerned, why we should refuse to consider the question, What are the qualities of an effective sermon? That is the topic which I have chosen for the present Lecture, but as I attempt to treat it, do not expect that I shall enter upon minute details concerning such technicalities as exordium, division, discussion, peroration, and the like. These belong to the work of the class of homiletics, and they have been already handled by a whole host of writers—by none more ably than by your own excellent Professor. You will not misunderstand me, either, if I should not repeat here what I have already said so emphatically about the importance of preaching " Christ and Him crucified." My present inquiry concerns not the matter, but the medium through which that matter is to be conveyed ; and my aim will be to give you a few general principles, emphasized by experience, which may guide you so to preach as to present the truth in the most winning and impressive form.

Now, in analyzing the qualities which go to make a sermon effective, I find some in the discourse itself, and some in the preacher, and though those which are in the sermon must have been first in the preacher, yet it will contribute to simplicity and tend to keep us from confusion, to adhere to this arrangement.

Taking those which are in the sermon itself, I name as the first, definiteness of aim. Every sermon should have a distinct object in view. One must preach, not because the Sabbath has come round, and he has to occupy the time somehow, but rather because there is something pressing upon his mind and heart which he feels impelled to proclaim. Some doctrine has taken hold of him with peculiar power, and while he is under the spell of it, he seeks to expound it to his hearers. Some phase of experience has come under his observation as he has been visiting from house to house, or has left its mark upon himself as he has been passing through it ; and while yet the impression is distinct, he makes it the theme of public discourse. Some sin has broken out with more than usual virulence in his neighborhood, and he sets the trumpet to his mouth that he may sound a timely alarm. Some department of Christian duty has been neglected by the members of his flock, and with all fidelity and tenderness he seeks to show them its importance, and to set before them the blessed results which would flow from their attention to it. And so as week after week revolves, each Lord's day's address has its distinct individuality since he has exerted himself in each to do one thing. This, as it seems to me, is the ideal of the ministry.

Ever, therefore, as you sit down to prepare your discourse, let your question be, " What is my purpose in this sermon?" and do not move a step until you have shaped out before your mind a definite answer to that inquiry. This will save you from that vagueness which chloroforms so many sermons and sends so many hearers to sleep. Set up your goal, and keep it always in sight, so every step you take will bring you nearer to its attainment, and your audience will be at no loss to see what you are driving at. The way to walk in a straight line over a trackless field, is to fix the eye, and keep it fixed, on some object that is stationary and sufficiently elevated, and then to move towards that ; and the great preventive of diffuseness and digression in discourse is to have, high above all other things in your mind, the perception of the purpose which your sermon is designed to fulfill.

But any purpose will not do. You must seek to have an aim whose importance will be sufficient to stimulate your own mind and to retain the attention of your hearers. Avoid all diminutive themes—such as may be discussed and settled in a few sentences ; for if you try to make a whole sermon on one of these, you will be tempted to fill up the time with vapid declamation, and will continue to spin away with the wheel of verbal fluency long after the " tow " of thought has been exhausted. That was a wise advice of Dr. James W. Alexander, " Preach on great subjects." There is something in them to inspire the preacher and to subdue and impress the hearer. Leave the lesser topics for minor occasions—such as the chair of the prayer-meeting or the table of the lecture-room will supply. But let your sermons be elevated in their subjects, and they will be elevating in their influence.

Yet, when you are dealing with a great theme, do not aim at being exhaustive. Leave something for again. Try, rather, to be clear, simple, instructive. You are not writing a treatise which is to contain everything that can be said on every branch of your subject ; you are going to address a company of fellow-men, to whom, in all likelihood, you will have many other opportunities of speaking, so let your endeavor be to give one distinct aspect of your theme, leaving other views of it for other occasions. I believe it is a common fault with young preachers to overweight their discourses with a superabundance of material. Their tendency is to put all they know on any subject into the discourse which is treating of that subject. So, in a very short time, they exhaust their own resources, and even before they have done that, they have exhausted the patience of their hearers. I well remember after I had preached my first sermon in a country church, there was reported to me a criticism which a plain, blunt man had made upon my discourse, which had a world of meaning in it in this connection. My text had been the first verse of the fifth chapter of the Epistle to the Romans, " Therefore, being justified by faith, we have peace with God through our Lord Jesus Christ," and I had dealt with justification, with faith, and with peace with God, as if I had resolved not to leave anything unsaid that could be said upon them. On coming out of the church, one of my hearers being asked what he thought of the discourse, replied, " These young preachers are like young delvers, they take thundering big spadefuls!" That witness was true, in my case, and I tried ever afterwards to lighten my discourses. Next to the evil of having nothing in a sermon at all, is that of having too much in it ; for in neither case does the hearer carry much away.

As another quality of an effective sermon I name precision of language. In a passage which I have already quoted it is said, " The preacher sought to find out acceptable words." He did not take the first which came ; but he selected those which best expressed his meaning, and were most suited to the people whom he was addressing. The relation of style to thought is of the closest kind ; and the aim of the preacher should be to get the clearest possible medium for the transmission of his thought. That is the best glass which most fully admits the light. The paintings which the artist produces are very excellent in themselves, but in a window they are out of place—if, that is, the end of the window is to let in the light. So, if the end of language is to transmit thought, then everything in it that withdraws attention from the thought to itself, or dims the lustre of the thought, is a blemish. Hence the preacher's study should be to have every sentence luminous with the thought which it is designed to express.

But how is that to be secured? Only, in my judgment, by the careful writing of every discourse. I have very strong convictions upon this point, and as a different opinion has been recently advanced by one whose views must be always received with deference and respect, you will forgive me if I seek, with some measure of fullness, to set forth my reasons for the advice which I have ventured to offer.

It seems to me that the importance of the work we are engaged in demands this exactness of written preparation at our hands. We are to speak to men about the most momentous matters that can occupy their attention, and a word thoughtlessly uttered may carry in it consequences of which at the moment we little dreamed. Nor is this an improbable contingency, for the right regulation of the tongue is the last attainment of Christian perfection. What says the apostle James? "If any man offend not in word, the same is a perfect man," and it is surely significant that this assertion of his comes in immediate connection with the injunction, "Be not many masters;" *i. e.*, teachers.* He would dissuade his readers from the consuming ambition to become teachers, by setting before them the difficulty that must ever be felt in regulating the tongue, which is the great instrument which a teacher employs. He, in effect, says that the διδάσκαλος attempts to perform the most im-

---

* The word in the original is διδάσκαλοι.

portant function, namely, that of instruction, with the most-difficult-to-be-managed instrument, namely, the tongue. But this suggestion, which was meant to dissuade the incompetent from pushing themselves into the teacher's office, is valuable also to those already in it, or preparing for it, as indicating to them a danger to which they are peculiarly exposed. It means for you and me, that we should take every possible precaution to secure that our public utterances shall be neither hasty, nor unadvised, nor of such a sort as shall bring reproach on the Gospel whose ministers we are.

Now the surest means of guarding against this danger is the use of the pen. Even those who advocate careful premeditation of the line of thought which the preacher proposes to follow, while yet the language is left to the prompting of the moment, insist that the constant practice of written composition is essential to success. But what is a young minister to write, if he do not write his discourses? He has not, except in very rare instances, the entrèe into the religious papers, much less into important magazines and Reviews. The request to contribute to these publications is commonly the consequence of a success already achieved, and so there is little prospect that he will be able to find continuous employment for his pen in any such way. How, then, is he to obtain it? Every student knows that while the love of truth may stimulate him to investigation, the incentive of some sort of publication is required to urge him to composition. But what kind of publication has in it more of inspiration for a preacher than that of the pulpit? To say, therefore, that a young minister should refrain from writing his sermons, and yet give himself to other compositions, is to bid him abstain from that which will most effectually furnish him for his work, while you commend him to other pursuits less fitted to give him the discipline he needs. If he do not write his discourses, the result, in ninety-nine cases out of every hundred, will be that he will write nothing at all, and then his sermons will become like Gratiano's reasons, having about a grain of thought to the bushel of words.

Moreover, as the minister is to speak on special themes, it is in reference to these subjects that he particularly needs to cultivate precision of language. But how will the composition of a literary essay give him definiteness of terminology, say for a doctrinal sermon, or even for a discourse exposing some prevalent evil or enforcing some neglected duty? Facility in sketching is very good, but that alone will not make an architect. To become an adept in that profession, one must study mainly the art of construction. Similarly the practice of composition in other departments will not make a man produce good sermons; that has to be learned by practice, and the thing to be practiced is the making of sermons.

But there is another reason why a sermon should be written out with care. We are able to secure thereby, that each portion of the discourse shall receive its due measure of attention. Even the most skillful extemporizers are in danger of enriching the earlier parts of their sermons at the expense of the later. They do not seem to have got quite above the fear that haunts the young orator, that he will never find enough in his theme to fill out the time allotted for his address, so they put a great deal into the introduction and the sections which immediately follow, and when they come to the closing portions, where all their resources should be brought into operation, they have no time left for the effective presentation even of the thoughts which they have premeditated, and are obliged to hasten over them so rapidly that the hearers lose all sense of their importance.

Repeatedly, as we have listened to such a preacher, we have seemed to ourselves to be driven by him up a long and winding avenue toward a spacious and hospitable mansion. But he has been diverting our attention ever and anon to interesting objects that line the way; here was an umbrageous elm, whose luxuriant foliage carpeted the earth with shade; there was an opening through which a beautiful glimpse of a delightful lake was seen, and yonder was a view of the distant mountains smoking under the sunshine. At length we reach the door of the house, but before we enter we have to survey the entire panorama from the piazza, and even as we pass through the hall we must pause a moment to admire some wonderful picture that hangs there; then, just as we gain a vision of the banquet which is laid out for us in the dining-room, we discover that we have barely time to reach the station so as to obtain the train for our return journey, and we have to leave the good things largely unenjoyed.

In a sermon of an hour's length I have more than once heard an introduction occupying five and twenty minutes; and on one occasion the preacher, not content with one introduction, made another as long as the first. Now, I do not say that such serious offences against the rule of proportion could not be committed in a written discourse, but I do affirm that they would be discovered, and opportunity would be afforded for their removal before the preacher attempted to submit it to the attention of his auditors.

Again, it ought not to be overlooked, that those extemporizers whose success is most frequently referred to as a reason why sermons should not be written, have generally had something which corresponded to sermon-writing after all. Thus in reference to Robert Hall, this testimony has been borne by Dr. Leifchild, who was his friend and neighbor in Bristol for some years: "I learned from him that most of his great sermons were first worked out in thought, and inwardly elaborated in the very words in which they were delivered. They were thus held so tenaciously in the memory that he could repeat them verbatim at the distance of years. He ridiculed the delusion of those who supposed that the perorations of his sermons were delivered impromptu, observing that they were the most carefully studied parts of the whole discourse." * Now this was composition of the most difficult kind, and was resorted to,

---

* A Memoir of Rev. Dr. Leifchild, by his son, J. R. Leifchild M.A., p. 137.

we may believe, because the physical infirmity with which Hall was afflicted made it agony for him to use the pen.

Again, in the case of F. W. Robertson; while it is true that he delivered his sermons without having written them, yet that is only half the truth, for he wrote them out on the Mondays after they had been preached, and thereby he had the "discipline of the pen" as really as if he had written them on the Fridays before they were spoken. If, therefore, his example is to be good for anything, it must be taken as a whole, for there is little doubt that as he looked back on what he had said, he would discover faults from which he would carefully abstain in his subsequent discourses. Nor should we fail to observe that if he had not written them, these wonderful sermons would have been completely lost to the world at large, and could not have been so widely useful as since his death they have become.

Similarly, in conversation with Mr. Spurgeon I once elicited from him the confession that the correcting of the proof of his Sunday morning sermon gave him, on every Tuesday, the same sort of wholesome discipline which we meaner mortals derive from the writing of our discourses. Only it gave it to him in a stronger measure, since faults always appear more glaring in the printed page than in the manuscript. He said that sometimes after he had gone over it with care the proof looked very black indeed, and though on such occasions he was apt to think that the reporter must have been asleep, he commonly discovered that the drowsiness had been in himself, and he was thereby stimulated to greater watchfulness in the future. But all such after-writing or correction is but " a light in the stern of the ship." The errors have been committed, and careful writing might have prevented their commission.

So again, when I hear my distinguished friend Dr. Storrs affirm concerning himself, that he has no verbal memory, and give that as a reason why in his preparations he cannot premeditate the words—which is only writing without the pen*—I am disposed to question the accuracy of his own self-judgment. I have read as a written article from his pen the very same words which, eighteen months before, I had heard from his lips in an apparently extemporaneous address, and I have heard it told that in a lecture delivered without notes, he gave, without either hesitancy or mistake, such a number of dates, that on the following morning a friend sent him a box of dates, accompanied with a note to the effect that " after the expenditure of the previous evening he judged he must be quite out of the article." These incidents, therefore, lead me to believe that, unconsciously to himself, that eloquent preacher has in his study so fixed his train of thought in his mind, that he has no difficulty in presenting it to his hearers in the very words in which he had before elaborated it. The recollection is so spontaneous that it seems to be

---

* See " Conditions of Success in Preaching Without Notes," by R. S. Storrs, D.D., LL.D.

reconstruction. But whether this be so or not, one must have his great mental excellences, and in addition, the drill of writing first-rate sermons for a quarter of a century, if he would faithfully follow the example which he has set.

It is, therefore, with the strongest conviction that I am giving you the best possible advice, that I say to you, write your sermons. This will give precision to your language more effectually than any other process, while when you are in an emergency and compelled to extemporize, some former train of thought will come at your call, clothed in the words in which you had before arrayed it.*

But I pass now to another quality of effectiveness in a sermon which is of not less importance than those already mentioned. I mean clearness in arrangement. In every discourse there must be method in order to movement, and one portion should succeed another in such a way as to carry forward the hearer gently yet inexorably to the conclusion. Arguments are like soldiers, they must be massed and marshalled in such a way as to overcome all opposition. Resting upon a broad base, they must be made to bring all their force to bear upon the main purpose which the

---

* " I should lay it down as a rule admitting of no exception, that a man will speak well in proportion as he has written much, and that with equal talents he will be the finest extempore speaker, when no time for preparing is allowed, who has prepared himself most sedulously when he had an opportunity of delivering a premeditated speech."—*Brougham's Inaugural Address as Lord Rector of Glasgow University.*

preacher has in view.   Like as in a pyramid, the figure rises, narrowing as it ascends, until it terminates in the apex ; so a discourse should become, step by step, more elevated, increasing in intensity as it rises, until it kindles into one burning point, and that point should be made to touch the soul of every hearer.   Or as in arch- ery, the marksman draws back the string on which he has fixed his arrow, in order that the full strength of the bow may go into the flight of the weapon, so the preacher should be all the while gathering energy for the truth which he designs at last to send quivering home to the heart of every hearer.   To this method of unity Jay has very seriously objected, affirming his preference for textual division ; but it seems to me that it is not impossible to combine the two.   And though it be true as he suggests, that "in preaching it should be remembered what diversities of persons and cases there are before us at every service, and how unlikely these diversities are to be reached by the very same thing," yet, it is not to be forgotten that in every good sermon which follows the plan of unity, the first part of the discourse gathers the hearers up and brings them together to the very point which is put before them at the close, so that each is made to feel that he has a personal responsibility in reference to it.   I have seen a shepherd gathering his flock upon the High- land hills.   He sent his trusty dogs far away out upon the mountain-side, and they, running round and round in ever-narrowing circles, brought the bleating multitude together, until each one in it was compelled to face the entrance into the fold.   So in a sermon, the earlier portions should be employed in encircling the audience, until at length, by the converging force of its ever-increasing pressure, the discourse brings each hearer up to the "strait gate," and compels him to face the question, " Shall I enter in ? "

The principles on which such an arrangement is to be made are set forth with sufficient fullness in the books on homiletics. Only let it never be forgotten that arrangement is essential to effect. It contributes to perspicuity. It helps the memory of the hearer to recall the various stages of your argument. It satisfies his judgment and carries him on without either effort or fatigue to a conclusion, which he feels to be a result, and not simply a cessation of speaking on your part.

When George Stephenson, the famous engineer, was beaten in argument by Buckland, and a few days afterwards Sir William Follett instructed by him, thoroughly vanquished his antagonist, he is reported to have said, that " of all the powers above and under the earth, there seems to be no power so great as the gift of the gab."* But I suspect that the burly engineer had mistaken the marshalling of arguments for the command of words. The great lawyer knew how to arrange his materials, and in that, rather than in his readiness of utterance, was the secret of his success. The nine digits may be so placed as to mean less than a unit, and, again, they may be put into such order as

---

* " The Life of George Stephenson and of his son, Robert Stephenson," by Samuel Smiles, p. 467.

shall mean a great deal. So it is with words and arguments, and he is the most effective sermonizer who makes every phrase, and illustration, and proof tell with all possible force.

Thus far, all are agreed, but there is a difference of opinion among authorities on the question whether this arrangement should be set before the hearers by the distinct announcement of the separate steps. On the one hand some have affirmed that "in many cases the divisions that are so formally announced are little better than a disguise of the heaviness of the discourse;"* and on the other it is alleged that "to the mass of hearers, concealed method is much the same as none."† It must be admitted, too, that the practice of formally giving out firstly, secondly, etc., has become rather unfashionable. Still it has many advantages to recommend it, but though it is my own general custom, my advice would be that you should not bind yourselves by any inexorable rule on such a matter. What is most of all to be avoided in the ministrations of the pulpit, is leaden uniformity. The sermon should never be stereotyped either in matter or in form. The preacher must vary his methods with judicious frequency; and while he has always the virtue of arrangement, he may sometimes allow it to exercise its force so irresistibly, that it will not need to be fore-heralded by announcement; and sometimes he may give out his heads without any danger of be-

---

* Blaikie's " For the Work of the Ministry," p. 184.

† Jay's " Autobiography," p. 138.

ing dull. It is not the announcing of the heads that makes a discourse heavy, but rather the fact that after they are announced, they are found to have no brains!

No man can be a sculptor without a competent knowledge of anatomy; but there is a marvelous difference between a skeleton and a statue. No preacher can succeed who has not in his discourse some principle of arrangement, but a syllogism is not a sermon. If the order is all in all, the discourse will be a syllabus; but if there be no order at all, it will be an aimless harangue; and in either case, it will be a failure. The guerilla soldier may now and then do a dashing thing, which harasses the enemy, and helps to secure success; but in a war the main reliance must be placed on the regular army, and for its operations order is essential. So, now and then an impulsive and energetic man may carry all before him by the force of mere explosiveness; but for constant effectiveness, there is nothing like method—only, the method must ever be your servant, and never your master.

I only add, in this connection, that a sermon, to be effective, must not be inordinately long. When weariness begins to be felt by the hearer, edification ends, and sometimes the latter portion of a discourse only effaces the impression which the earlier has made. No matter how many other excellences a preacher may have, they will all be neutralized if he habitually err in this respect. Even such eloquence as that of Edward Irving could not hold an audience Sabbath after Sabbath for the two hours and a half which he was resolved "he would have the privilege of;" and there is such a thing yet in the pulpit as flailing away at over-threshed straw, until the ears of the hearers, deafened by the din, seek refuge in the unconsciousness of sleep.

But while we condemn inordinate length as fatal, it does not therefore follow, that brevity is in and of itself an excellence. "How long did I preach?" said a young man to the venerable pastor whose pulpit he had been occupying for the morning. "Just twelve minutes," was the response. "I am glad of that," replied the elated freshman, "for I never like to be tedious." "O! but you were tedious," said the old man, with a quiet irony, which extinguished him. It is possible for one man to be even more dreary in ten minutes, than another would be in an hour and a half; and in these days when the demand is that discourses shall be measured off by the hourglass, as the merchant disposes of dry-goods by the yard, and when it is almost an unpardonable sin if a preacher shall require the attention of his audience for more than thirty minutes, we need to give emphasis to the truth that the length of an address, whether in the pulpit or elsewhere, ought to be determined by the nature of the subject to which it is devoted. If that can be clearly opened up and faithfully enforced in twenty minutes, then there is no need to take more; if, however, that cannot be done in less than an hour, then, even such an amount of time should be cheerfully conceded to it. The preacher should stop when he has reached a conclusion; that is, when he has brought his arguments and illustrations to such a focus that the truth he means to establish is burned in on the souls of those whom he addresses. If he go on after that, his continuance is an impertinence; but if he end before that, his sermon is a fragment, and will lead to no result.

In this view of the case, few things are of sadder omen for the churches than the unreasoning clamoi for brevity in sermons which is so universal among the people; for if the pulpit is to be the place of instruction, he who speaks from it must have a certain latitude given him, in the matter of time, in order that he may be faithful to the trust which has been committed to him. The teacher of chemistry, or of ethics, or of political economy, or of social economics, is allowed ample scope when he comes to the platform; and as the minister is also the teacher of the doctrines of the Word of God, the same privilege ought to be accorded to him. Let any one attempt to unfold the Scriptural truth about faith, or repentance, or the atonement, or justification, or regeneration, or eternal judgment, or even any one aspect of these subjects in fifteen minutes, and he will see how utterly hopeless his undertaking is. So if we are shut up to a certain statutory allowance of so many minutes, the results will be that doctrinal instruction and systematic exposition of the sacred Scriptures will be banished from the sanctuary, and we shall train a generation of spiritual infants, to whom it may be said that "when for the time they ought to be teachers, they need that one should teach them again what be the first principles of the oracles of God."*

---

* Hebrews v. 12.

Men may make themselves merry, indeed, over the long sermons of our Puritan forefathers, with their ninthlies of the thirteenth head, but we should not forget that those who relished the discourses of Howe, and Owen, and Baxter, were the strong heroes who won the liberties of England, and the near kinsmen of the noble pilgrims who laid the foundations of this republic. Depend upon it, if ever the pulpit shall cease to be a vehicle of instruction, and sink into a place for the public reading of pretty little essays, or the utterance of fifteen minutes of rose-water sentimentalism, our people will dwindle into spiritual dwarfs, and the manhood will disappear from their piety.

Of course, there is a proper medium to be observed in this as in other matters, and we must never forget that while brevity is not in itself considered a mark of excellence, inordinate length will mar the force even of the noblest production. We must teach men " as they are able to bear it," and if we are dealing with great subjects in a way to interest and instruct the hearers, a little common sense will be of more use to us than any rigid rule in determining the length of our discourse. He who is saying nothing, cannot have done too soon. He who is saying something, will always say that best in the fewest words. When the nail is driven home, all after-hammering is superfluous ; but if we stop before we have driven it home, we might as well never have begun to drive it.

LECTURE VI.

THE QUALITIES OF AN EFFECTIVE SERMON—IN THE PREACHER.

LECTURE VI.

THE QUALITIES OF AN EFFECTIVE SERMON—
IN THE PREACHER.

IN speaking of the qualities of an effective sermon, so far as these are in the preacher, I shall not refer to literary culture or elocutionary skill, though these in their own places have an importance not to be overlooked; but I shall confine my attention to those spiritual elements of power which have their source in the convictions and character of the minister himself.

And foremost among these I name earnestness. But wherein does earnestness consist? The question is by no means unnecessary, for the term has become one of the " cant " words of the time, and in the frequency of its use we are apt to lose sight of its true significance.

We must not confound it with mere vehemence of manner. Rant is not intensity, neither is noise earnestness. Too often the " sound and fury " signify " nothing;" and sometimes as I have been compelled to listen to preachers of the noisy school, I have thought that they had taken their cue from Quince in his description of the lion's part, when he says, " You may do it extempore, for it is nothing but roaring."* That is, and always must be, ridiculous,

---

* Midsummer-Night's Dream, Act I., Scene II.

and the antics which such orators cut remind me of
the position once occupied by a dignified professor
of divinity, when, being in a boat with a party, and
thinking he could row with ease, he took an oar,
and at the second or third stroke " caught a crab,"
so that he lay sprawling, hands and heels uppermost,
in a most ludicrous plight, and was thus addressed
by his venerable mother, " Less pith, and more to
the purpose, my man !"   Let the " pith " be all " to
the purpose," gentlemen, for it is in the purpose first
and always that the earnestness must lie.   It is not
a manner which can be put on from without, but an
influence, say, rather, an effluence, which must ema-
nate from within.   It cannot be acquired by any practice, or successfully imitated from any model.   Neither can it be simulated by any process.   It is part
of the man.

It springs out of an unwavering conviction of the
truth of that which we are at the moment preaching,
and of the fact that just that truth needs to be spoken
to our hearers.   If we have not made up our minds
upon a subject, we cannot kindle into enthusiasm
over its treatment ; and he who has not yet brought
the ends of his thoughts together on any matter,
should keep that matter out of the pulpit until he
has.   It is the irrepressible in a man that makes him
earnest.   If he can keep anything in, then let him
keep it, for such a thing, generally speaking, is not
worth letting out, and his utterance of it will have no
force.   But when it comes to such a point with him that
he feels like the old prophet who said, " His word was

in mine heart as a burning fire shut up in my bones, and I was weary with forbearing, and I could not stay,"* then he will speak in such a way as to thrill and overawe his hearers. When, like Peter before the council, he is as if under some inner impulsion, and says, " I cannot but speak,"† or when, like Paul, he cries, " Necessity is laid upon me, yea, woe is unto me if I preach not," then his earnestness will come as a thing of course, and there will be as much difference between his words and those of the mere rhetorician, as there is between the mimic thunder of the theatre and the reverberations of the cloud-artillery as they are redoubled by the Alpine echoes.

In the lack of this, as it seems to me, we have the secret of the easy nonchalance, not to say indifference, which many hearers complain of in the ministrations of the modern pulpit. The preacher fills up the time with talk, because he must *say* something. He does not go into the sacred desk under the absorbing impulse of the feeling that he has something which he *must* say. So he is aimless and uninteresting, and fails to impress others because he is unimpressed himself. It cannot be too constantly remembered by you, that your usefulness to others must depend, next to the influence of God's Spirit, upon the intensity of your own convictions. There is nothing so contagious as conviction. The perception that you are well assured of the truth of that which you affirm, will help your hearers into the same

---

* Jeremiah xx. 9.   † Acts iv. 20.

certainty; and often in the times when their faith is sorely tried and is almost ready to fail, their observation of your confidence will lift them into trust. Their reliance on you will lead them to believe in what you say. But if you devote your sermons to the enumeration and illustration of the things which you do not believe ; if you are careful only to discuss the points on which you are either undecided or out of harmony with other and more ordinary men, you will produce anything but conviction, and will win from the more intelligent of your hearers the criticism pronounced by Johnson on Dr. Priestley, " He unsettles everything and settles nothing."

If, therefore, you have no positive convictions, keep out of the pulpit until you get them ; and when you get them, they will make for themselves a manly and earnest utterance. Do not, I beseech you, enter upon a pastorate professing, in a fashion, to hold certain truths which yet are not such to you, as that you feel you *must preach* them at all hazards. Such a position will be fatal to usefulness. Shape to yourselves clear and definite views regarding " the truth as it is in Jesus," and let the measure of your love to Him be that also of the firmness with which you hold them ; so shall the fervor of your affection for your Lord inspire and energize your utterances. " We, having the same spirit of faith according as it is written, I believed, and, therefore, have I spoken, we also believe and therefore speak."* Mark the force of that

---

* 2 Cor. iv. 13.

" therefore ;" it is the hinge on which all true earnestness turns ; without that your words will be little
better than "drowsy tinklings ;" with that they
will be full of force, and you will be like him of whom
the poet* speaks, as on a "throne mounted in heav-
en," and shooting "into the dark, arrows of lightening."

But another element of earnestness is a vivid realization of the position of our hearers. Let a man
have the firm belief that he is dealing with immortal
souls ; that unless these souls embrace the Lord Jesus
Christ and live in obedience to His laws, they must
perish everlastingly ; and that he is set to persuade
them to choose that "good part which cannot be
taken away" from them, and he cannot help being
earnest in his appeals to them.

When one reads in the biography of that great and
good man after whom this lectureship is named, that
his six sermons on "Intemperance" were preached
in order that he might save some of the members of
his congregation whom he most tenderly loved, from
the horrible hell of the drunkard, we have at once
the explanation of their scorching earnestness and of
their irresistible power.

In the same way we account for the fiery logic of
the Epistle to the Galatians. The apostle saw that
the truth of the Gospel was endangered, and that those
beloved ones over whose conversion he had rejoiced
were in the greatest peril, and so he sat down, and with

---

* Tennyson.   Sonnet to J. M. K.

his own hand he wrote to them, in large letters, that epistle wherein " the arrows of his thoughts " are " headed and winged with flame." Here is the explanation of its passionate energy, its scathing invective, its rapid movement, its parental tenderness, and its condensed power. He saw them in danger, and he was in haste to rescue them. His one great aim was to open their eyes to their real position, and to bring them back to the security that is in Christ. I do not say that he was not in earnest in all his epistles, but we cannot read that letter without feeling that he was peculiarly moved when he penned it, and as a consequence it peculiarly affects us.

Now, from the difference between that and his other writings, we may learn much regarding the earnestness of which we are in search. Especially we discover that the perception of the circumstances of those to whom we speak, will give us such concern for their welfare that we shall lose sight of all things else in the effort to secure their salvation. There is no mistaking the earnestness of him who runs from the burning dwelling to cry " Fire! fire!" He sees the evil ; he knows that if means be not taken promptly to extinguish the flames the house must be destroyed ; and so he does not take it leisurely, but rushes on along the nearest way to the engine-house. And it is the same in the pulpit. When the salvation of souls or the benefit of men in some special direction is the uppermost object in the preacher's ambition, earnestness will come unsought ; but without that it can never be attained.

A Summer or two ago, a clergyman of the Church of England, who was taking a holiday in Switzerland, came, in one of the mountain passes of that land, to a place of considerable danger, and as he was threading his way with care, he heard a piercing shriek, which, at length, he found proceeded from a lady, who was down on the side of the precipice in a position of awful peril, and who was crying for assistance. Taking a hasty survey of the situation, he went by what seemed to him the best way to her relief, and after making great efforts, he succeeded in bringing her with him to a place of safety. The next day he went with a friend to show him the spot, but though he tried very hard, he found that he could not get anywhere near it. Would you know the reason of this difference? In the former instance there was *a life to be saved;* in the latter there was only a display to be made. Let not the lesson be lost upon us. We shall always do most, my young brethren, when we are directly seeking to save souls; but when we are working only for display, we shall inevitably fail. If you keep your eye on the end to be gained, you will be sure to be earnest; but when you attempt to show how you have done it, or how you can do it, the earnestness will evaporate.

Think, then, ever as you enter the pulpit on the position and necessities of your hearers. See in them a company of fellow immortals, each of whom is needing your help in the great struggle of life, and in your eagerness to assist them, all thoughts of self will die out of your soul. Your hearts will be filled with yearning affection for them, and that itself will be a power over them, for as one* has said :

> " If mountains can be moved by faith,
>   Is there less power in love ?"

All your words will be made to converge toward the great result on which your heart is fixed; and your ministry, as a whole, will grow in interest under your eyes, as you watch week by week for the effects of your labors.

Here, then, are the twin sources of that earnestness of which so much is said, namely, intellectual conviction of the truth of those things which we proclaim; and loving realization of the fact that our hearers need to have these things said to them in order to be saved from the evils of time and the perdition of eternity. Give us these in all the occupants of all our pulpits, and the world will be constrained to listen to them. There is no royal road to earnestness; neither can it be successfully counterfeited by any histrionic art. We can gain it only through personal conviction and pervasive love; but, when we do gain it, we do not so much possess it as it possesses us, and carries us out of ourselves to achievements which are as astonishing to ourselves as they are irresistible to those whom we address.

A second quality of effectiveness in the preacher is courage. It is said of the apostles that "they spake

---

* Frederick William Faber.

the Word of God with boldness ;"* and all who since their days have been signally successful in the winning of souls have been distinguished by the same characteristic. They have "not shunned to declare all the counsel of God."† They have used "great plainness of speech," calling things by their right names, and exposing, when need was, the evils which existed in the Church, in the home, and in the community. John of the golden mouth would not have been so blessed to the citizens of Antioch and Constantinople, if he had not been so fearless in his denunciations of corruptions, no matter in what rank of society they appeared ; and if Luther had not possessed " the spirit and power of Elijah," the Reformation from popery had not resulted from his labors.

It may seem strange that I should connect such great names as these with the enforcement of the cultivation of courage upon you, but even if your lot should be cast in the humblest village, let me assure you from my own experience, that it will require as much heroism to breast the tide of antagonism there, as it does in the largest city. "The fear of man bringeth a snare ;" therefore, when you enter the pulpit, let all considerations of personal comfort or interest sink out of sight, while you seek to enforce upon your hearers that which is "right in the sight of God." If you are determined only to set forth the truth of God, you may rely upon it that God will take care of you.

---

* Acts iv. 31.   † Acts xx. 27.

I say not, indeed, that you are at liberty to indulge in personal invective in your discourses. If you have anything against any individual among your flock, " go and tell him his fault between thee and him alone;" but be not guilty of the cowardice of attacking him in the house of God, when he has no opportunity of reply.   Impertinence is not faithfulness, and rudeness is not Christian courage.   If you mean to do good to a man, the very worst course you can take is to begin by insulting him.   Be as fearless as you please in the denunciation of sins, but take care that you do not so describe an individual sinner as to enable all your hearers to identify him. Men come to the house of God to be preached *to*, not to be preached *at*, and your aim should be to secure that each auditor shall make application to himself of the truth which you are enforcing.   Generally speaking, the hearers of our discourses are inclined of themselves to be amazingly benevolent with our words, and will, without any help of ours, give them all away among their neighbors.   It is not for us, therefore, to pander to that tendency by striking plainly at certain individuals.   Our duty rather is to concentrate the thoughts of each upon himself, so that the one arrow which we send forth, may, by the power of the divine Spirit, be multiplied to the piercing of a thousand hearts.

But while we avoid all invidious personalities, we must be careful not to keep back any part of the truth from the fear of offending any prominent individual, or provoking " Demetrius and the craftsmen."

We must preach the preaching that God bids us, "diminishing not a word ;"* and if men will take offence, we must see to it, that the cause of their indignation shall be in the truth itself and not in our manner of proclaiming it.

Now there is only one way of securing this, and that is by cultivating faith in the unseen presence of Christ with us. We must preach as Moses endured,† "as seeing Him who is invisible." That will both lift us above the fear of men and keep us from saying anything which would be inconsistent with his precepts and example. We complicate matters so soon as we begin to ask, What will this man think? or, How will that one feel? or, Will not this seriously affect my future comfort? or the church's financial condition? In each of these directions humiliation and failure lie. Our safety is in the consciousness of the presence of Christ. There will be no difficulty about what we ought to say, or how we ought to say it, so long as we think of pleasing Him, but the moment any regard to self-interest intrudes, embarrassment begins.

Moreover, if we yield to these selfish temptations, we are sure in the end to miss the comfort which we have been seeking. "He that loveth his life" thus, "will lose it,"† for the timid trimmer who is always trying to keep from offence, becomes at length an object of contempt; while he who faithfully reproves, rebukes, and exhorts with all long-suffering and doctrine, becomes a power in the community, and draws

---

* Jeremiah xxvi. 2.   † Hebrews xi. 27.   ‡ John xii. 25.

to himself the confidence and affection of his people. The sycophant is despised even by those on whom he fawns, but he who speaks to men in the assurance that God is with him, will secure both their attention and respect, even when he is telling them unpalatable truths. John the Baptist was popular just because he was pungent; and the most attractive preachers of our own days are those who are most courageous in their antagonism to existing evils.

But even if that were not the case, it would still be our duty to keep back from our hearers nothing that will be profitable unto them; to seek their good, rather than their good opinion; and to set clearly before them the solemn responsibilities of life. This is demanded of us alike by loyalty to God, a regard for the welfare of those who wait upon our ministry, and a consideration of the account which we ourselves must give. To each of us God says as He did to Ezekiel, "O, son of man, I have set thee a watchman unto the house of thy people; therefore, thou shalt hear the word at my mouth, and warn them from me. When I say unto the wicked, O, wicked man, thou shalt surely die; if thou dost not speak to warn the wicked from his way, that wicked man shall die in his iniquity; but his blood will I require at thine hand."* When we remember *that*, and have besides the consciousness that he is near us who has said,† "Lo I am with you always, even unto the end of the world," the fear of man will be banished by the desire to

---

* Ezekiel xxxiii. 7–8.   † Matthew xxviii. 20.

serve God, and there will be that about us which will make our hearers feel that it is with God, rather than with us, that they have specially to do. "The Lord God of Israel, before whom I stand," said Elijah when he confronted Ahab, and in these words we have the open secret of his dauntless demeanor. Let us stand consciously in the presence of the living God when we are in the pulpit, and every other feeling and fear will be overmastered in the determination to be faithful to Him in the service of our people.

The minister's bearing should be in keeping with the words of Paul, "I am not ashamed of the gospel of Christ, for it is the power of God unto salvation to every one that believeth;"* and when he feels in that way, he will be ready to preach it anywhere, whether in the centres of intellectual culture and fashionable refinement, or in the haunts of wickedness, where Satan has his seat. When we begin to apologize for the truth, or in any way to lower the flag of Him whose messengers we are before the arrogance of the world, our influence is on the wane. But with courage in our hearts, the battle is half won, even before we enter the lists; and when men see our boldness, they will "take knowledge of us that we have been with Jesus. †" Our bodily presence may be "weak" and our "speech contemptible," but our boldness, if it be seen to spring from our conviction that God is with us, will be itself a sermon, and will make men say regarding us, as was said of an humble Scottish pas-

---

* Romans i. 16.   † Acts iv. 13.

tor, "That man preaches as if the Lord Jesus Christ was at his elbow." So preached the first apostles, and so must we if we are to have repeated among us the blessings of Pentecost or the successes of the early Church.

But as another element of effectiveness in the preacher, I name tenderness. It may be thought by some that this is thoroughly incompatible with courage, but in reality it is only its complement. Without tenderness the courage would stiffen into harshness. Without courage the tenderness would degenerate into tepid sentimentalism. In the union of the two, we get the highest excellence of both; the tenderness shading the courage into loving faithfulness; and the courage giving principle to the tenderness, so that its manifestation is in harmony with rectitude. How admirably these qualities were blended in Paul! We think of him usually, indeed, as the stern reprover, the dauntless hero, the uncompromising champion of truth, but there were in his soul great fountains of tenderness, which ever and anon overflowed in tears. Thus he tells the Thessalonians that he was "gentle among them" as "a nurse cherishing her children;"* and when he was constrained in his letter to the Philippians† to testify against some who were "the enemies of the cross of Christ," he did so, "even weeping." So also among the Ephesians,‡ "by the space of three years he

---

* 1 Thess. ii. 7.   † Phil. iii. 18.   ‡ Acts xx. 31.

ceased not to warn every one night and day with tears." Now there is no doubt that in this gentleness lay much of his power.

And he was, in this respect, only the follower of the Lord Jesus himself. How tenderly He dealt with the Pharisaic Nicodemus, as well as with the woman at the well! How lovingly He received the publicans and sinners when they came unto Him! How like a mother with her children He was in His training of His disciples, teaching them as they were willing to be taught, dealing with them often in the way of indirectness, and having ever as the background even of His reproofs, His love, shading and softening its severity; yet, singularly enough, making it thereby only the more effective. Truly, by " His gentleness " He made them "great." And, if we would educate our people into lives of holiness, we must imbibe His spirit.

Many men are all courage, and many are all tenderness. But few combine them in one and the same address, yet that is what is most needed in our pulpits in these days. We want the amalgamation of the two, for the tenderest things are then most apt to stir up to practical reformation when they are uttered by one whose courage has not flinched from the proclamation of God's law; and the sternest things are then the strongest, when the tear-drop quivers in the eye of him who utters them. When, therefore, we are in the tender mood, we ought to give good heed that we manifest courage; and when we are dealing in the terror of the Lord, then is the time to cultivate peculiar tenderness.

But how shall we acquire this gentleness? There is but one answer, by remembering what we were ourselves, and how God dealt with us. Very suggestive here, to us all, is the case of John Newton—great, strong man that he was, but with a heart as tender as his intellect was vigorous.* Jay tells the following story of an interview with him: "When I one day called upon him, he said, 'I am glad to see you, for I have just received a letter from Bath, and you may know something of the writer,' mentioning his name. I told him I did, and that he had been for years a hearer of mine, but he was a most awful character, and almost in all evil. 'But,' said he, 'he writes now like a penitent.' I said, 'He may be such, but if he be, I shall never despair of the conversion of any one again.' 'Oh!' said he, 'I never did since God saved me.' And the same authority informs us that on the wall of his study at Olney, just over his desk, he had in very large letters these words, "Remember that thou wast a bondman in the land of Egypt, and the Lord thy God redeemed thee." Who can doubt that in the spirit which prompted him to put these words there, we have the secret of his power in dealing with hardened sinners? and the source whence flowed those Cardiphonia which have so refreshed every reader of his works. When Jesus healed the leper, He touched him, and thereby He did as much good to the poor man's soul as to his body; "for here" might the outcast sufferer have said, "is

---

* Autobiography and Reminiscences of the Rev. William Jay, pp. 275–277.

one, and He the purest of them all, who is not ashamed to come into contact with me." So if we would benefit men we must come into heart contact with them. But how is that to be accomplished? Let our common speech instruct us. We say of a tender utterance, that it is "touching." So, by the hand of gentleness, we touch the soul of the hearer, and if we be ourselves in sympathy with Jesus, having our other hand of faith in His, there will be healing in the touch. "Virtue will go out of us," and in the strength of that, the sinner will be encouraged to seek his Saviour.

But no make-believe gentleness will produce such effects. To be thus operative our tenderness must be true. The falsetto of the melodrama has no efficacy in the pulpit. The tear that drops upon our Bible must be sincere;* and so again we come back to those elements of earnestness on which already I have so fully insisted, for only when we are intensely convinced of the truth of what we say, and have a vivid realization of the circumstances of our hearers, can we be really compassionate.

"And Jesus saw a great multitude, and was moved with compassion toward them."† How often, as I have entered my pulpit, have these words come rushing into my heart; and if I have been in any degree successful in comforting the sorrowful or directing the perplexed, or strengthening the tempted, it has been because I have tried to take for my motto as a

---

* See Cowper's Eulogy of Whitefield in his poem on Hope.
† Matt. xiv. 14.

preacher the words of my Master, " I will not send them away fasting, lest they faint in the way." *

The nearer you keep to Him, and the more closely you study the necessities of your people, the more easy will it be for you to be gentle toward them. Never forget that they are always needing help ; and remember always, that you are the servant of Him of whom it was said, " A bruised reed shall he not break, and the smoking flax shall he not quench." Then tenderness will come to you as the habit of your Christian life, and will give its soft and searching undertone to all your words.

But I have said nothing in all this regarding the manner of delivery ; and I have not touched upon the vexed question of the use of the manuscript. Nor is there any necessity that I should go at any length into the consideration of such matters. Given burning earnestness, unflinching courage, and sympathetic tenderness in the preacher, and those other things may be very safely left to take care of themselves. He who is characterized by these three qualities, will very soon come to the discovery of what is best for him, and will ultimately concentrate his energies on the doing of that effectively. One man here, cannot lay down the law for another ; neither ought one man to cavil at or condemn the practice of another. The preacher who rivets the attention of the hearer, and moves his heart, and leads him for the

---

* Matt. xv. 32.

moment to forget everything but the truth which is set before him, has thereby vindicated his own excellence, no matter what plan he has adopted. That a manuscript must necessarily impair the power of a speaker, cannot be successfully maintained in the face of such cases as those of Edwards and Chalmers. That free speech must always promote efficiency in the pulpit, will not be assented to by those who are condemned to listen from time to time to men who are more remarkable for fluency than for force. A discourse may be delivered with as little animation or fervor as if it had been read with the most slavish closeness; and another may be read with as much freedom and fire as if it had been delivered.

Abstractly, of course, there can be no doubt that free speech is the normal method for the pulpit. Yet, a question like this is not to be settled on mere abstract principles; and the very fact that different ways have been adopted by different men, all of whom were first-rate preachers, is a proof that no one mode can be declared to be the only best. Some, having written their discourse fully, commit it to memory, and deliver it verbatim. This plan has been supposed by many to involve tremendous drudgery; and I suppose that they who so speak regarding it, would find it to be a dreadful task. But, having myself practiced it for the first ten years of my ministry, I can attest that it did not in any degree hamper me. " The memory," as Jay has said, " is like a friend, and loves to be trusted," so that the labor of an hour and a

half came with me to be sufficient for the mastery
of a discourse that was newly-written; and I own
to a feeling of regret that I ever gave up the practice.
Still, I found that the more carefully I had prepared a
sermon, it was the more difficult to commit it to
memory; and as it was just then that I wished to
give it with verbal accuracy, I was led to put the
manuscript before me, and use it as occasion required.
After I had done that a few times, I discovered that
I had lost my facility in remembering, and so, ever since,
having no aptitude whatever for extempore speech, I
have endeavored to train myself to use a manuscript
with effect. If I might speak from my own experience, therefore, I would say, that *memoriter* preaching is the method which has the greatest advantages,
with the fewest disadvantages; extempore preaching is the method in the employment of which success is hardest, and failure commonest; and preaching
from a manuscript is the method in which, if he choose
to train himself in it, the man of average ability will
make, on the whole, the best of his talents, and make
the fewest failures. There are not above half a score
of men in a century who can rise to the foremost
places for usefulness and eminence through extempore speech. If you be one of these, there will be in
you that irrepressibility which is the mark of genius,
and which will force itself out at length against every
obstacle. If you be not one of these, then, with all
respect to those who I know differ from me on this
subject, I do not hesitate to say, that it will be ten

times better for you, and a thousand times better for
your hearers, that you should educate yourself into
the free and unfettered use of a full manuscript.

Observe what I have said, "educate yourself into
the free and unfettered use of a full manuscript." I
do not mean that you should keep your face close to
the desk, and never lift your eyes from the page
unless it be to look right up into the ventilator that
is overhead; but that you should *preach* from your
manuscript. Write in a fair, round, legible hand;
marking the beginnings of your sentences, and the
different stages of your argument in such a way that
your eye may easily catch them. Spend a couple of
hours with your manuscript before you enter the pulpit, seeking to catch the spirit of your theme and to
kindle under the enthusiasm of your words. Do not
disdain to attend to such little matters as the folding
up of the corner of each page, so that you may turn
it over without hindrance. And above all, remember
whose messenger you are, and what you design to
attain through the special message which you mean
to deliver. Rise to your work from your knees, and
then your manuscript will be no more a hindrance to
you than its wings are to the bird, or its sails are to
the ship. It will help you to rise; it will give energy
to your movement; it will give calmness to your soul
even in your most impassioned moments, and before
you have gone on many minutes, your hearers will
forget alike the manuscript and yourself in their
solemn appreciation of the truth you speak.

Make your choice of the method which suits you

best, seek to do your best in that method, and do both out of regard to Jesus and the souls of men. It is not the manuscript that either makes or mars efficiency, it is the man behind it. If he be cold, the absence of the paper will not make him warm; but if he be on fire, the paper, as in the case of Chalmers, may only make the blaze the stronger.

LECTURE VII.

EXPOSITORY PREACHING.

LECTURE VII.

EXPOSITORY PREACHING.

BY expository preaching, I mean that method of pulpit discourse which consists in the consecutive interpretation, and practical enforcement, of a book of the sacred canon. It differs, thus, from topical preaching, which may be described as the selection of a clause, or verse, or section of the inspired Word, from which some one principle is evolved and kept continuously before the hearer's mind, as the speaker traces its manifold applications to present circumstances, and to human life; from doctrinal preaching, which prosecutes a system of Biblical induction in regard to some great truth, such as justification, regeneration, the atonement, or the like, gathering together all the portions of holy writ that bear upon it, and deducing from them some formulated inference; from hortatory preaching, which sets itself to the enforcement of some neglected duty, or the exposure of some prevalent iniquity; and from biographical preaching, which, taking some Scripture character for its theme, gives an analysis of the moral nature of the man, like that which Bishop Butler has made in his wonderful discourse on Balaam, and points from it lessons of warning or example.

But, though thus distinct from each other, these several methods of pulpit discourse are not inconsistent with each other. Into every sermon exposition must, in some degree, enter. It must, indeed, form the foundation on which every discourse must be reared, if, at least, it is to be a sermon proper, and not a mere essay, or lecture, such as one may hear at an ordinary Lyceum. Moreover, into the regularly maintained expository series, all these other elements of topical, doctrinal, hortatory, and biographic interest will come, if only the preacher will intelligently follow the course of argument or narrative taken by the inspired writer whose work he is seeking to interpret. Practically, therefore, the *differentia* of the method of preaching of which I am now to treat, is its continuous and consecutive character, giving, as it does, a connected view either of a history or a treatise.

Now, on the very threshold of our plea, let it be distinctly understood, that I do not advocate this mode of discourse to the disparagement or neglect of all others. He who desires to be an efficient minister will endeavor in his public teachings to combine them all. My own practice has been, for many years, to give up one of the services of each Lord's day to the systematic exposition of some book of Scripture, leaving the other free for the presentation of such subjects as may be suggested to me by the occurrences of the times, or the circumstances of my people. This division I have felt to be not only very convenient, but also extremely serviceable. You will remember, therefore, that in my after-remarks I do not desire to exalt expository preaching above all other varieties of pulpit discourse, far less to urge it upon ministers and students to the neglect of every other method. But, as it seems to me that this mode has fallen somewhat into reproach and disuetude among us, I wish to speak a few earnest words in favor of its revival and more general adoption.

Exposition is the presentation to the people, in an intelligible and forcible manner, of the meaning of the sacred writer which has been first settled by the preacher for himself, by the use of those grammatical and historical instruments with which his preparatory training has furnished him. It is not the mere dilution of the statements of the sacred writer by the repetition of his thought in language necessarily less forcible than his own, for that would make it only a weak and watery paraphrase of the original. Neither is it the learned and exhaustive enumeration of all the interpretations which commentators, ancient and modern, have given of it. Still less is it the utterance of a few pious platitudes in the way of inference from it. But it is the giving of a simple statement of the writer's meaning, with the grounds on which the explanation rests, and the lessons which it suggests whether for " doctrine, reproof, correction, or instruction, in righteousness." It is the honest answer which the preacher gives, after faithful study, to these questions, " What is the mind of the Holy Spirit in this passage ? and what is its bearing on related

Christian truths, or on the life and conversation of the Christian himself?" If it be an argument that is before him, he will analyze it from its premises to its conclusion, noting the different steps in the process, marking the illustrations with which it is accompanied, and pointing out its pertinency to the primary purpose of the writer, as well as emphasizing its permanent importance in the department of doctrine or of duty. If it be a narrative, he will, by the help of the historical imagination, seek to give it vividness by reproducing the times and circumstances to which it belongs; then going beneath the surface, he will endeavor to discover those principles of the divine administration which it illustrates, and so he will find in the inspired record of the past the explanation of the present; and in some degree also the prophecy of the future. If it be a parable, he will try to obtain the key to its interpretation, in the purpose for which it was spoken, or in the occasion out of which it sprung, and then he will give unity to his exposition, by making everything in it subservient to that, guarding on the one hand against the spiritualization of every minute particular, and on the other against the merging of everything into a vague and dreamy generality. If it be a prophecy, he will seize the central position of the seer, and group every detail around that, remembering evermore that " the testimony of Jesus is the Spirit of prophecy." In a word, he will study thoroughly those inspired expositions of portions of the Old Testament which are given in the Epistles to the Galatians and Hebrews, and those infallible models of parabolic interpretation which the Great Teacher Himself has furnished, and he will endeavor to apply the principles on which these are constructed to all similar portions of the Word of God.

In dealing with historical subjects, special attention should be given to the vivifying of the record by the reproduction of the surroundings. People are apt to forget that the Bible heroes were men of like passions with themselves; and we should endeavor to give humanness to them in all our descriptions. The visitor to the Ceramic gallery in the South Kensington Museum, reads on the etchings of each window the history of the formation of the articles in the section beneath it. He gazes with interest on the Chinese productions, and as he looks up he sees upon the window a representation of Chinese potters at their toil. He admires the singular ware made by Palissy, and as he raises his eyes he sees on the window the image of the persevering Huguenot, feeding his furnace with the broken furniture of his cottage, against the protest of his pleading wife. Now, what that luminous framework is to each case in that interesting exhibition, a vivid reproduction of the scenes and circumstances of sacred history is to the characters of the men that moved in them, and to the truths which were proclaimed in connection with them. It is the appropriate setting to the precious stone. It hangs the picture in a frame that is itself luminous and instructive. And treated thus with vigorous imagination and practical purpose, the Bible becomes the most living, the most interesting, and the most stimulating of books.

To do all this well, however, it is evident that great labor will be needed, while the attempt will furnish occasion for the employment of some of the noblest of our intellectual powers. It requires a lively imagination; a calm, unbiased judgment; a correct scholarship, and a true homiletic instinct, to lay every thing under tribute for purposes of instruction and edification. Added to these, a large acquaintance with modern literature will enable the preacher to give interest to his discourses by pointing out the parallels which secular history presents to that recorded in the Book of God, or by furnishing him with striking illustrations drawn from science or art, from nature or from the works of man.

The method to be pursued in expounding a book of Scripture will vary with the nature of the book itself, or with the purpose of the expositor. In general, however, it will be well for him before entering upon such a work to read the book through, if possible, in the original language. Then, he will endeavor to divide it into its different sections, mapping out his course thus from the first. Then, as each of these portions falls to be considered, he will study it carefully, seeking to find some principle of unity in it, around which he may crystallize his different propositions. Then, with this, his own method in his mind, and having first satisfied himself as to the meaning of the section, he will read all that his library contains upon the subject (and for the purpose of reference, if he be wise, he will construct an index to his library, entering upon an interleaved Bible a citation of the name and page of every book opposite the verse or chapter of which it treats). Then, having thus saturated his mind with the subject, and seen what others have said upon it, he will leave it all to simmer and settle for some days, and, at length, sitting down with his whole soul concentrated upon the work, he will produce a discourse which, by the blessing of God, will be at once interesting and instructive, stimulating and suggestive to his hearers. Thus from week to week he will go forward, his spirit kindling into increasing enthusiasm as he proceeds, so that he will forget the labor in the joy. His people, also, catching fire from him, will long for the return of the Lord's day, that they may renew their study with him, and will deeply regret when by sickness, or absence from home, they are deprived of one of the series. I have seen a slimly attended second service gather back into itself all the half-day hearers that had absented themselves from it, and draw in others besides, through the adoption by the minister of just such a method as this ; while the effect, even upon those who have dropped casually in upon a single discourse, has been to send them away with what one of themselves called " a new appetite for the Word of God."

I am thus brought naturally to the consideration of the advantages which are connected with this method of ministerial instruction, and among these I mention, First, the fact that *it brings both preacher*

*and hearers into direct and immediate contact with
the mind of the Spirit.* The open Bible on the sacred
desk is the token that both speaker and auditors regard it as the ultimate standard of appeal. In the
pulpit the minister is not, ordinarily speaking, dealing
with those who repudiate the authority of the Word
of God. The very presence of his people in the
sanctuary may be taken by him as an admission that
"they are all present before God, to hear what is
commanded them of God." There may be exceptional occasions when he feels bound to deal with
sceptical objectors, but, as a general rule, the pulpit
is not the place for that. As a brother once said to
me, "When I am in the pulpit, I am not there to
defend the Bible; the Bible is there to defend me."
The great aim of the preacher ought to be to set
before the people the mind of God. Now, in so far
as he is successful, that is precisely what the expositor
does. In the topical sermon, there may be many of
his own particular opinions, which are matters of
"private interpretation," or of "doubtful disputa-
tion." But when he has succeeded in convincing his
hearers that he has given the true meaning of the
passage which he is expounding, he can say, "This is
the mind of Christ," and the force of that both on
him and them will be overwhelming. When he so
speaks, he will speak "with authority and not as the
scribes," and men will feel that they have been
brought face to face with God.

Now, it is in the production of this impression that
the peculiar power of the pulpit consists. Other men

have genius, and can produce wonderful results by the flashes of its erratic lightening. Other men have stores of information on which they can draw at will, and with which they can enrich their utterances. Other men have force of logic and power of invective, by which they can bear down all opposition. But, so long as the preacher is wielding these alone, he has not risen to his distinctive office, and is not clothing himself with his own peculiar power. That which gives him the might over men which every true preacher ought to wield, is that he can show that he has the Word of God behind him. Unless he can impress that upon his hearers, he is no more to them than the political orator or the literary essayist. Unless he can make men feel that it is not so much with himself, as with God, that they have to do, the most superb mental endowments will not enable him to secure the great end for which his office has been instituted ; but if he has been successful in conveying that impression he has proved his fitness for his work, even if he have no grace of oratory or charm of diction. " By manifestation of the truth to commend ourselves to every man's conscience in the sight of God "—that is our work as ministers of the Gospel ; and if through the neglect of the exposition of the Word of God, or through the deceitful handling of that Word, we fail to use the power which is distinctively our own, we shall be like Samson shorn of his locks, and may, by and by, descend so low as to make sport for the Philistines of our generation. Hence, as the special engine of the preacher's influence, I advocate most earnestly the systematic exposition of the sacred Scriptures.

A second advantage of this method is, that *it secures variety in the ministrations of the preacher.* Every man has his own peculiar idiosyncracies, and, yielding to these, he will be attracted more strongly and more frequently to some subjects than to others. Unless, therefore, the preacher pursue some regular course of exposition, he will be in danger of confining himself to a few favorite themes, and ringing the changes upon them, until his hearers become weary both of him and of them. But if he follow the course of some book, or trace out consecutively the chapters of some sacred biography, he will discover the same old truths, with ever fresh surroundings, and will secure that variety in unity, which is the charm of God's book of revelation as much as of His book of nature.

It is the same Mont Blanc which the traveller sees from the bridge of Sallanches, from the summit of the Col-de-Balme, and from the sweet seclusion of the Valley of Chamouny. But each of these points of view brings new features into prominence, which have a special fascination of their own. So it is the same truth of justification that we look on in the Epistles to the Romans and Galatians, and in the general Epistle of James; but in each we have some feature that we have not in the others; and as we contemplate that, we have an interest which the others failed to awaken in us. Some time ago, in visiting an English colliery, I was shown, in the office, a beautiful scale of the different strata through which they had sunk the shaft some 300 fathoms deep. It was very interesting, and gave me a good idea enough of the geology of the place; but when, a few days after, walking out with my friend, we came on a peculiar-looking, up-jutting rock, I learned something about the nature of the underlying treasures which the table in the counting-house had failed to teach. Now, that perfectly illustrates the difference between systematic theology and Biblical, exposition. In the former, you have everything arranged by the scale; in the latter, you come upon truths *in situ*, and there is much of interest in the discovery, and of instruction in the surroundings.

He who preaches merely on the general topic of regeneration, must treat it in a more or less stereotyped fashion; but let him, in the course of his expositions, come upon such a passage as that in the beginning of Peter's first epistle : " Blessed be the God and Father of our Lord Jesus Christ, which according to his abundant mercy hath begotten us again unto a lively hope by the resurrection of Jesus Christ from the dead ;" or such an one as that in the first chapter of the Epistle of James: " Of his own will begat he us by the word of truth, that we should be a kind of first fruits of his creatures," and he will, as a conscientious interpreter, be compelled to look at related topics in such a way as to give new interest to the great central subject. Is it impertinent in me, brethren, to suggest that the neglect of exposition may have something to do with the brief average duration of pastorates among us, concerning which so many regrets are expressed? The merely topical preacher will very soon wear himself out, because he is drawing simply on his own resources all through. But the expositor has the Word of God before him, and his life-time will not exhaust that. As he follows the discourses of Jesus, or the reasonings of the Apostles, or the devotional meditations of the Psalmist, the infinite variety of these utterances will keep him from running into ruts of thought, or expression, or topic, and he will be like the well-instructed scribe of whom the Master speaks, " Bringing out of his treasure-house things new and old." I have heard a venerable minister tell that Dr. John Dick, the well-known professor of theology in Scotland, went, in the early days of his ministry, to a neighboring clergyman in the deepest distress, saying to him, " What shall I do? I have preached all I know to the people, and have nothing else to give them. I have gone through the catechism, and what have I more?" To which his friend replied, " The catechism ! `Take the Bible, man. It will take you a long while to exhaust that." For variety and suggestiveness, for fullness and inexhaustibility, there is no book like the Bible. Make it, therefore, your constant theme, until the people call you as they did Luther, Doctor Biblicus, for that is the most worthy degree a minister can earn.

A third advantage of this method is that in following it out *the preacher will be compelled to treat many subjects from which otherwise he might have shrunk*, but which ought to be dealt with by him, if he would not "shun to declare all the counsel of God." Every pastor knows that there are almost always some members of his congregation who specially need to be enlightened on some points of duty, or of danger. But if he were to select a subject purely for them, his object would be defeated, because they would be apt to suspect him of deliberate intention to strike them, and would resent that which they felt to be a preaching *at* them, rather than *to* them. Now, in following a regular course of exposition, opportunities are continually furnished to us for the presentation of timely truths, while no one can say that we have gone out of our way for the special purpose of reaching his conscience.

Besides, there are whole classes of topics which would be completely ignored by us if we were to be guided only by our own tastes and feelings in the choice of subjects. One man would dwell exclusively on doctrinal matters to the neglect of the practical. Another, catching the modern infection, would sneer at doctrine, and present subjects without connecting them in any remotest manner with the cross of Christ. One would deal constantly with the love of God, as if there were no other text in the Bible than the glorious declaration that "God is love." Another would be forever dwelling on the justice of God's government, as if there were no fatherly heart in Him who rules the world. One would descant unweariedly on the sovereignty of God, and be forever preaching on the subjects of election and fore-ordination, forgetting the gracious invitations which are addressed to all. Another, in his eagerness to press home these invitations, might ignore the agency of the Holy Ghost, and so do dishonor to the Comforter. And thus, in spite of themselves, perhaps, indeed, unconsciously to themselves, each would give a defective presentation of truth.

Half-truths are always the most insidious forms of error, and it is to be feared that many of the half-truths which are so popular in these days, have had their origin in the neglect of a thorough and systematic expository treatment of the Word of God as a whole. By following the plan which I am advocating, however, we would, in course of time, go round the whole globe of revealed truth, and learn to preach each doctrine in its own proportion, or, as Paul has phrased it, "To prophesy according to the proportion of the faith." *

So, again, we should be led to distribute our attention fairly between the different books of the Bible itself. A venerable minister used to say that there were always sounding in his ears the cries of neglected texts of Scripture, saying to him, "Won't you show how important we are?" So, I often think, I hear the complaints of neglected books of the Word of God. You would be astonished at the result, if only for twelve months you were to keep a register of the texts that are preached from in any one of our sanctuaries. How limited is the area within which we

---

* Romans xii. 6.

confine ourselves in the selection of subjects! Some are constantly in the Old Testament; others appear to think that the Jewish Scriptures are of no use to us. Many are passionate in their devotion to the psalms; and some see no beauty in them that they should be desired. The Gospels are the special favorites of some, and the Epistles are too frequently ignored by all. Now it is not safe to neglect even those books of Scripture which seem to be the driest and least interesting. We should not forget that it was from the apparently uninviting pages of the book of Deuteronomy that our Lord Jesus drew those weapons with which He foiled the adversary in the wilderness; and if we will only enter upon the work with a devout heart, and an earnest spirit, we may find the richest interest and the rarest profit, in some, at first—shall I say repulsive?—portion of the Word of God.

Thus, take the history of Nehemiah. Most people would be inclined to pass it by. They would extend to the book, as a whole, the criticism pronounced by a Scotch woman upon the tenth chapter of it under the following circumstances. Her husband was reading that portion of Scripture at family worship, and as, in the failing light of the Summer evening, he had some difficulty in making out the proper names which it contained, he said, "Jenny, woman, bring a candle!" "'Deed, no!" was the answer; "the loss would be more than the profit, with that chapter, ony way!" But I can testify from personal experience, that one of the most interesting and profitable series of discourses which I have ever preached, was founded on that book. Sometimes the soil which is most rugged on the surface, covers the richest veins of ore ; and, not unfrequently, the most beautiful flowers are seen growing out of the crevices of the rock. Thus it is with many of the neglected books of the Bible, for if we will only dig beneath the surface of them we shall discover many mines of wealth, and by going through them all, we shall make ourselves "thoroughly furnished unto all good works."

Then it must not be forgotten that in expounding thus, we make our hearers sharers with us in our privileges.

So, as a fourth advantage of this method, I name the fact that *it will promote Biblical intelligence among our people*. Those who have not investigated the matter will be surprised to find how limited an acquaintance many church-goers have with the sacred Scriptures. They may be acute in business, and well "up" in all matters of politics, while yet they have never carefully perused many portions of the Word of God. There are whole books of the Bible which to many worshipers in our pews are as much an unexplored territory as is the interior of the continent of Africa. Ask them to find the prophecy of Zephaniah, and see what work they will make of their search ! They know the Gospels tolerably well, but they do not care very much for the Epistles ; they may have read many of the Psalms again and again, but they have little acquaintance with, or relish for, the historical or prophetical books of the Old Testament.

When, some eight or nine years ago, Mr. John Bright, with that happy talent for giving appropriate names by which he is distinguished, spoke of Mr. Robert Lowe and his friends, who rebelled against the Reform Bill of the liberal leader, as having gone into a cave of Adullam, two country members of the British House of Commons were overheard conversing thus, as they were leaving the Chamber of Parliament: " I say, where did Bright get that illustration of his to-night about the cave?" "Oh," was the reply, " I see what you're up to; do you suppose I haven't read the 'Arabian Nights'?" And yet these men were tolerably fair senators, according as senators go. I am persuaded that most of us overrate the Biblical knowledge of our hearers, and that it would be of immense consequence to them, as well as to ourselves, if we should give ourselves to the consecutive exposition of the Scriptures. Even if the Bible were nothing more than a valuable human production, its earnest study would tend to develop mental vigor and moral strength. But when we take its divine inspiration and beneficent purpose into consideration, it becomes infinitely more important that we should concentrate our attention more thoroughly upon it. Men in the parlor, in the closet, and in the counting-room, are overlaying the Word of God beneath the mountain of new books that are forever issuing from the press; therefore, in the pulpit, we ministers should more and more exalt it, and seek to increase at once the acquaintance of our hearers with it, and their reverence for it. Truth is the nutriment of the soul, and Bible-truth is the stamina of the spiritual life. It gives strength and stability to Christian character, and he who is familiar with it is not easily moved from the path of duty, or lightly "tossed" by every wind of doctrine. The great defection of the Ritualistic party in the Church of England was preceded by a depreciation of the pulpit. The preacher forgot that his mission was to instruct, and so substituted a few minutes of vapid sentiment for an earnest effort to expound the Scriptures. Biblical intelligence is absolutely essential to doctrinal steadfastness and Christian stability. It is as true now as when the Psalmist wrote, that he who medidates in God's law day and night, shall be "like a tree planted by the rivers of water that bringeth forth his fruit in his season ; his leaf also shall not wither, and whatsoever he doeth shall prosper."*

As a final advantage of this method, I mention the fact, that *in the process of preparing his expository discourses, the preacher will acquire a great store of materials which he can use for other purposes*, and, in particular, will have constantly suggested to him fresh subjects for topical sermons. Max Müller has entitled his essays, "Chips from a German Workshop," indicating that the materials of which they are composed were struck off in the elaboration by him of his more systematic works ; and the readers of the "Greyson Letters" are conscious that they consist of the fragments that remained after

* Psalm i. 3.

the composition by its author of " The Eclipse of Faith." Now, much in the same way the Biblical expositor is obliged, week after week, to put aside a great many valuable and suggestive thoughts for which he can find no appropriate place in his regular lectures, but which he can use either in the illustration of other discourses or in the construction of topical sermons. " Reading," as Lord Bacon says, " maketh a full man ;" and the continuous study of the holy Scriptures, and of the works of others on them, cannot but fill the mind with ample stores from which the minister will be always drawing with advantage both to himself and to his hearers.

In the preparation of the ordinary sermon, he is working out of a treasury which he has already acquired ; in the study of his expositions, he is constantly laying up new stores. Every week he gathers far more than he can give in any one discourse ; but that which he is compelled, for the time, to reject, remains with him as a constant possession, and in due season is brought forth to enrich the minds of his people and influence their lives.

In this way, too, he will be saved from that most horrible of all drudgeries, the " hunting for a text ;" for he will have always at hand a host of subjects which have been suggested to him, and when he chooses one, he will take it, not from a sense of constraint because he must preach upon something, but with a feeling of satisfaction, because he has something which he must preach upon. For many years, in my own ministry, I have never known a time when

I had not in my mind a large number of subjects, each of which was, as it were, eager to receive my first attention, but which I was compelled to detain, that it might wait its turn; and so the question has been, not What can I get to preach on? but rather Which one of many topics has the most pressing claims and the most immediate interest? Now, I trace the existence of this state of things to my constant habit of expository preaching on at least one part of every Lord's day.

But an example will be to students and ministers worth far more than any mere general statement here, so perhaps I may be allowed to give one chapter from my recent experience. It is my duty to prepare notes to the "International Lessons" for one of our religious papers, and in the course for the three opening months of last year, I had occasion to go into the histories of Joshua and the Judges. These books are not generally accounted the most suggestive for homiletic purposes. Yet, after having done what I could to help the Sunday-school teachers, there remained on my own hands the following sheaf of valuable texts, some of which I have already preached on, and others are waiting only for a favorable opportunity. From the lesson on the crossing of the Jordan I got the phrase, "Ye have not passed this way heretofore," suggesting the topic how to meet unknown difficulties; from that on the sin of Achan I got the evil influence of one man's sin on others, founded on the words, "That man perished not alone in his iniquity"; from that on the division of the land I got

the expostulation, " How long are ye slack to go to
possess the land which the Lord God of your fathers
hath given you?" which may be used either as enforcing efforts after the attainment of personal holiness or as stirring up to home missionary zeal; from
that on the Promise broken I got the words, " They
followed other gods of the gods of the people that
were round about them," which may be employed as
the starting-point of a discourse on conformity to the
prevailing fashion of the world; from the story of
Gideon I got the phrase, " Faint, yet pursuing ;" and
from the history of Samson I obtained the clause,
" Samson wist not that the Lord had departed from
him," which, taken in connection with the parallel
statement regarding Moses, that " he wist not that
the skin of his face did shine," suggested as a subject
" the element of unconsciousness in character." Other
expositors I know would have been drawn to other
topics ; but no man whose business it is to preach,
could go over these chapters earnestly and prayerfully without having some fruitful themes suggested
to him ; and thus, far from being inconsistent with topical preaching, the habit of exposition will give new interest to that also, and will enable the minister to
present old truths with constant freshness and variety.
Hence, apart from the advantages which the people
derive from it, I could not afford to give up my habit
of " lecturing," as we Scotchmen call it, because of its
influence on my own mind and heart.

But, in reply to all my arguments, it will be said,

" Expository preaching is not popular. The people do not like it, and they will not stand it." Now, in answer to this, I have to say that the minister has to consult the benefit of his hearers as well as their tastes; and where the two conflict, he has to prefer that which will promote the former rather than that which will please the latter. If he is fully persuaded that they need such instruction as Biblical exposition regularly prosecuted can alone impart, then he ought to give himself to it, even at the risk of creating some little dissatisfaction at first; for he may rely upon it, that if he do his work faithfully and well, they will grow interested in spite of themselves, and will come at length to enjoy it. Of course, if he is ambitious of acquiring a reputation for " great sermons" and wishes to hear many complimentary expressions about the beauty and brilliancy of his " effort," then he will leave off exposition, and indeed in that case, he had better leave off preaching altogether, for the pulpit is not the place for such displays. But if he wish to honor God's truth, and if his desire be to hear his people tell him that they have never before so thoroughly understood some portion of Scripture, or that his explanation of a passage has taken a stumbling-block out of their way or put a staff of strength into their hands, he will go on with his expository work, content; oh, much more than content! rejoicing in the fact that he has been in any smallest degree the instrument of building up the Christian character of the people of his charge.

But why is this sort of preaching not popular ? **Is**

it not because those who have attempted it have done so too often without any adequate idea of its importance, and have gone on with it in the most slovenly and perfunctory fashion? They have been content to "say away" on the passage, or, to use an expressive Scotch word, they have "perlikewed" awhile, going about it and about it, until everybody hearing them has been longing for the amen. They have taken to exposition because they thought it was an easier thing to do than to write sermons, and they have simply diluted the sayings of the sacred writer by the watery additions of their extempore, not to say ex-trumpery, utterances. They have had recourse to it with the feelings of him who said, "I like to take a whole chapter for a text, because when I am persecuted in one verse, I can flee to another."

Now of course that is fatal. Such preaching does not deserve to be popular, and it is a proof of the good sense of our people that it is not popular. Let no man who wishes to succeed in exposition imagine that he can do so without great labor. No mere cursory perusal of the passage before he goes to the pulpit will suffice. No hasty study of it will be enough. He needs to enter into the spirit of the writer, to recall the times and circumstances in which he wrote, and to live and move and have his being for the week in the argument or narrative, the prophecy or parable, the psalm or supplication, which he is considering. He must follow the old canon of Bengel: "Apply thy whole self to the text, and apply the whole text to thyself." Thus will he discover the "hidden treasures" in the field of sacred Scripture, and when he speaks of them to his hearers, his words will have in them that unmistakable ring—that "accent of conviction," as Mullois calls it—which will make every one feel that he is in living earnest.

One thing, however, he must guard against. He must not turn the pulpit into the chair of the exegetical professor, and spend a long time in hunting down some poor Greek particle, or digging up some obscure Hebrew root. Processes are for the study; results are for the pulpit. Our people do not want to know what every German, English, or American commentator has thought. When one asks what time it is, it would be a mockery of his request if you should begin to tell him all the details of the mechanism of a watch, or if you should go into an exhaustive dissertation on the relative merits of Trinity church clock, or Bennet's, or the clock at the railway depot. You look at your own watch and tell him what its fingers point to, and that is all.

So let it be here. Do not make your expository lecture a place of deposit for barrowfuls of other men's opinions, gathered from all quarters, but tell your hearers what you have concluded for yourselves, with the grounds on which your opinion rests, and then pass on and press the practical application of the principle which you have found in the passage to the consciences of your people and the circumstances of your times.

That this kind of preaching will be both profitable and popular has been clearly proved, both from the past history of the pulpit* and from the success of many living preachers. Let the young minister, therefore, take courage and labor on at it. Above all, let him remember here, as in all other things, his dependence on the Holy Spirit, and prayerfully seeking that in the closet, while he diligently does his best in the study let him go forward in the confidence that he will succeed, for God hath said, "Them that honor me, I will honor."

Not all at once will the success come. But it will come as the result of these three things: prayer, perseverance, and patience. Keep on, therefore, with resolute courage, for "all things are possible to him that believeth."

---

* For illustrations, I might point to Dr. John Dick's Lectures on the Acts of the Apostles; Dr. John Brown's volumes on the Discourses and Sayings of the Lord; the volumes by Dr. Hanna on The Life of Christ; those of Trench and Arnot on the Parables; the various works of Dr. Cox, now editor of the *Expositor ;* and for separate passages, "An Expositor's Note-Book," by the author last named. The volume of Robertson on the Corinthians and those of Vaughan on the Philippians and the book of Revelation are exceedingly valuable, while in another style Peddie's Jonah and Raleigh's Jonah are admirable.

LECTURE VIII.

ON THE USE OF ILLUSTRATIONS IN PREACHING.

LECTURE VIII.

ON THE USE OF ILLUSTRATIONS IN PREACHING.

IN its widest sense, illustration includes everything which is employed for the purpose of making an argument intelligible, attractive, or convincing. In recent times, however, it has been virtually restricted to such rhetorical figures as the metaphor, the simile, the allegory, and the parable. When, therefore, I speak of the use of illustrations in preaching, it will be understood that I employ the term in its narrower and more modern application as equivalent to similitudes.

Now, in the outset, it is important to say that illustrations ought not to form the staple of a sermon. There must be something to be illustrated. In former days, preachers were exceedingly sparing in their use of comparisons; but under the influence of the example of such men as Guthrie, Beecher, and others, a great reaction has set in, and the danger now is that discourses shall consist of illustrations, and nothing else. But the beauty of a simile lies in its pertinence to the point which you design to brighten by its light. Without that, it has no business in your discourse. When illustrations will help to make your argument more simple, they are to be used with discretion; but when they are employed purely for the sake of the stories of which they consist, and to hide the poverty of the thuoght, they are a snare to the preacher and an offence to the hearer.

Much of the Sunday-school oratory of these days is vitiated by this false rhetoric, and there are many among us who would agree with the German lady from whose diary Mr. Spurgeon has quoted the following sentences: "There is a mission station here, and young men come down to preach to us. I do not wish to find fault with these young gentlemen, but they tell us a great many very pretty little stories, and I do not think there is much else in what they say. Also, I have heard some of their little stories before; therefore, they do not so much interest me as they would do if they would tell us some good doctrine out of the Scriptures." *   Be sure that you have the good doctrine in full prominence, then let the light of your illustrations fall on that and you will be safe. Repeatedly, however, have I heard incidents introduced into discourses which, though interesting enough in themselves, had no bearing, either immediate or remote, on the subject which the preacher was professing to discuss. They simply filled up time, and by diverting the attention from the topic which ought to have been uppermost, they did more harm than good. Remember, therefore, that as it is essential to a good style that one should

---

* "Lectures to my Students," by C. H. Spurgeon. English Edition, p. 147.

have something to say, and should say that well; so it is no less essential to the proper use of illustration that one should have something to illustrate, and should use his simile in such a manner as to illustrate that well. We may paint a picture, but we must never do that for the sake of the picture. That must always be subordinated to the truth which the analogy is meant to illuminate.

This principle was once emphasized to me in a very suggestive way. Spending a few days, some years ago, in the quiet little English town of Lutterworth, where I was refreshing my spirit with the memories of Wycliffe, I went into the shop of a cabinet-maker, where I saw a magnificent book-case which had just been finished for one of the gentry of the neighborhood. I was at once attracted by it, and began to examine it minutely. Then I ventured rashly to criticize it, and even suggested something which I thought would be an improvement. But the intelligent workman said, " I could not do that, sir, for it would be contrary to one great rule in art." " What rule?" I asked. " This rule," replied he, " that we must never construct ornament, but only ornament construction." It was quaintly spoken, but it was to me a word in season. I saw in a moment that this principle held as truly in the architecture of a sermon as in that of a cathedral—in the construction of a discourse as in that of a book-case; and often since, when I have caught myself making ornament for its own sake, I have destroyed what I had written, and I have done so simply from the recollection of that artisan's reproof. There is a whole "philosophy of rhetoric" in his words. Whenever, therefore, you are tempted to let illustration become the principal thing, or to forget the great object of your discourse, in your effort to work in the drapery of some beautiful image, let this good rule come back upon you with its wholesome counsel. See that you have construction to ornament before you allow ornament to make its appearance.

But, presuming that you have in your discourse a body of substantial thought, or that it consists mainly of a closely-linked argumentative chain, what is the use of illustration?

To this question several answers, all equally true and equally important, may be given.

In the first place, it helps to make your thought clear. This, indeed, must be suggested by the very etymology of the term. An illustration must mean that which throws light in upon something else. It is to a thought, or an assertion, or an argument, what a window is to a room, letting the brilliancy of the sunlight in upon it, and making every portion of it luminous. It uses that which is known and acknowledged to be true in such a way as to lead the hearer's mind to the acceptance of something else of which he has heretofore been in doubt. It employs the imagination for the assistance of the judgment. Nay, frequently it brings the material to the aid of the spiritual, and by the clear analysis of the visible it helps the soul to see that which is invisible. For example, if one should have a difficulty in assenting to the words of James, " For whosoever shall keep the whole law, and yet offend in one point, he is guilty of all;"* we might help him to its acceptance by a simple statement and illustration, thus: The principle that we are bound to obey God, by whom it was enjoined, is that which underlies the law as a whole; hence, he who violates one precept of it does thereby abjure that authority by which they are all alike enforced. Thus the commandments of the law are like a necklace of pearls from which one cannot be torn away without breaking the string on which all the others are threaded with it, and letting them fall ignominiously to the ground. In this way material things are used as a diagram for the demonstration of spiritual, and they who apprehend the point of the analogy have no longer any hesitation about the statement.

But there is more than an illuminating power in a good illustration. It has a force of proof as well. As one has very well put it, " Wherever similes rest on the unity between God's world and man's nature, they are arguments as well as illustrations." † This was clearly seen and readily acknowledged, even by such a philosopher as Sir William Hamilton, who vindicated his liking for the illustrative preaching of Dr. Guthrie in these words, " He has the best of all logic; there is but one step between his premise and

---

* James ii. 10.

† Dr. John Ker's Reminiscences of Dr. Thomas Guthrie in Autobiography and Memoir of Guthrie. Vol. II. p. 359.

his conclusion." * Even our ordinary speech may in-struct us here, for there is an intimate connection between the "like" and the "likely." The similitude is in and of itself a ground of probability; and in modern science many most important discoveries have been suggested by analogy. The poetic insight of the physical philosopher leads him to the percep-tion of hidden analogies through which he rises to the apprehension of new truth. And the same genius in the preacher leads him to see the correspondencies which God has made between the material and the spiritual departments of His universe, and to use these for the attainment of the great ends of his calling. The world of nature came from the hand of Him who made the soul of man; and the administration of Providence is carried on by Him who gave to us the revelation of His will through the sacred Scriptures. We may expect, therefore, to find a principle of unity running through them all. Milton was giving utter-ance to a correct philosophy, as well as true poetry, when he said,

> " What if earth
> Be but the shadow of heaven, and things therein
> Each to the other like, more than on earth is thought."

This is the principle that gives the Saviour's parables all their power. They are something more than felicitous illustrations. They are outward symbols of inward realities, and the laws that obtain in the

---

* Dr. McCosh's Reminiscences of Guthrie. Autobiography ut sup Vol. I., p. 322.

one were felt by his hearers to be operative in the other. Whether He drew His analogies from human life or from external nature, He so employed them as to make them effective for demonstration as well as for elucidation. They proved as well as illumined the truth. As Trench has said, " Their power lay in the harmony unconsciously felt by all men, and which all deeper minds have delighted to trace, between the natural and spiritual worlds, so that analogies. from the first are felt to be something more than illustrations, happily, but yet arbitrariiy, chosen. They are arguments, and may be alleged as witnesses : the world of nature being throughout a witness for the world of spirit proceeding from the same hand, growing out of the same root, and being constituted for that very end." *

We may not claim the same force of argument for every analogy which we discover; but in so far as the analogy is true, the illustration which we employ has such an influence, and even when it may fall short of establishing a probability in favor of that which we are seeking to prove, it is invaluable, as Bishop Butler has clearly shown, in answering objections. Frequently a striking analogy will do more to convince the wavering, and to establish the weak in faith, than a whole volume of philosophic argument ; and so

----

* " Notes on the Parables of our Lord." By Archbishop Trench, pp. 12, 13. The whole section from which these sentences are taken is pre-eminently worthy of the young preacher's study.

even as a means of persuasion, the study of the art of illustration is as important as is that of logic.

But, leaving the rationale of illustration, I pass on to observe that the employment of similitudes is of great service in awakening and sustaining the interest of an audience. Here, again, etymology vindicates our position. Just as the " like " leads to the " likely," so it is that for which we have a " liking." Every one is delighted with a vivid and effective illustration. It is to a sermon what the picture is to the school-book of the little child. The lesson is made agreeable by means of the drawing. The thing may be over-done, indeed, and the art may be something of the clumsi-est, but still the little student will read to find out what the picture means. And in the same way the hearer will listen to learn what you are going to make of your analogy. While you are dealing with the story, he is all attention, and it will be your own fault if, before his interest flags, you have not insinuated your lesson, or pointed your application. Look at the parables of the great Teacher, and you will dis-cover how, while yet in the absorption of their atten-tion, His auditors had left the gates into the citadel of " Mansoul " unguarded, He entered before they were aware, and made His application in such a way as thrilled them through. Often He made them judge themselves, and, sometimes, when they had pronounced sentence on the character and conduct which He had depicted, He turned upon them as Nathan did on David, saying to each of them, " Thou art the man."

This is an incidental advantage from the use of illustration which is often of great importance. Many of our hearers come to the place of assembly prejudiced against the truth, and by the wise employment of some beautiful or touching analogy, we may so disarm them for the moment, that before they have time to resume their antagonism, we may, by the help of God's Spirit, secure an entrance for the truth into their minds. They become interested in spite of themselves; and when their attitude is most intense, then is our time to strike. If Nathan had gone to David with a direct denunciation of his iniquity, the monarch might have been tempted to drive him from his presence. But the parable fascinated him, and then the prophet could speak to him as strongly as he pleased.

Moreover, the impressions which are thus produced are never forgotten. You may find difficulty in recalling an intricate argument; but you will be sure to remember that which was fastened to an illustration. Hence, if you wish your discourses to be memorable, you will seek to have them aptly illustrated. When Guthrie began his ministry at Arbirlot, he instituted a Bible-class, which met every Lord's day immediately after the service, and one part of its exercises was the going over, catechetically, of the discourse which he had just delivered. At first he was surprised to find that his pupils remembered so little. But, perceiving that they always easily recalled an illustration, and the truth which it was meant to illuminate, he was led to give special attention to that source of pulpit

efficiency, and so he began that course which culmi-
nated in his after greatness. Now, we may profit
much by this experience. We may not all become
Guthries, indeed. It is not desirable, either, that we
should. But we shall each become more admirably
furnished for the glorious work to which we have consecrated ourselves; and our words will be both
winged and weighted; flying far, yet fixing themselves permanently where they fall. But we need not
deal in amplification here; the whole truth upon this
matter has been condensed for us by one who was
himself a master in the art, into these sentences,
which at once explain and exemplify its advantages:
" The chief and common object of a parable is by the
story to win attention and maintain it; to give plainness and point, and, therefore, power to the truth.
By awakening and gratifying the imagination, the
truth finds its way more readily to the heart and
makes a deeper impression on the memory. The
story, like a float, keeps it from sinking; like a nail,
fastens it in the mind; like the feathers of an arrow
makes it strike, and like the barb makes it stick." *

But, you ask, how are we to get illustrations? And
in answer to that inquiry, I begin by saying that if
I may speak from my own experience, there is no
faculty which is more susceptible of development by
culture than that of discovering analogies. When I

* " The Parables, Read in the Light of the Present Day." By
Thomas Guthrie, D.D., p. 9.

commenced my ministry, it was a rare thing with me to use an illustration. My style then was particularly argumentative, and my aim was to convince and satisfy the understanding, and then to make my appeal warmly to the heart. But shortly after my removal from my Scotch parsonage to Liverpool, Guthrie's Gospel in Ezekiel was published, and this was followed a few months later by Mr. Beecher's Life Thoughts. These two books opened my eyes to see what was lying all around me. Under the inspiration which they communicated to me, I began to look for spiritual analogies in everything. The books I read ; the places I visited ; the incidents that passed under my observation ; the discoveries of science with which I became acquainted—all were scanned by me for the purpose of finding in them, if possible, something that might be used in pulpit illustration. And so it came that when I sat down to my desk, appropriate analogies would rise to my pen, and the difficulty was not how to get illustrations, but which to choose out of the many that offered themselves for my purpose. It might have been easy to have saved myself all this trouble, if I had been content to have appropriated ready-made the analogies employed by those eminent preachers to whom I have referred, or to have availed myself of those helps to laziness which have been published in the shape of Cyclopædias of Religious Anecdotes and Illustrations. But not to speak of the dishonesty of such a proceeding, there would have been nothing in all that to educate me into the discovery of similitudes for myself. So I used these books, rather as suggesting to me how I should go to work for myself, than as store-houses out of which I might help myself as occasion required.

While, therefore, I recommend you to study very closely the illustrations of other men, let me urge you, also, to make your own for yourselves. Even if no one in your audience should know that your analogy is not original, there will be in your own soul, while you are giving it, a feeling of meanness which will prevent you from using it effectively; so that when you do employ the illustration of another, it would be well always to acknowledge it. But it is a thousand times better for you to make your own. Look for them. I might paraphrase here the inscription on the monument of Sir Christopher Wren, " *Si illustrationes quæris circumspice.*" You will find them in the talk of the children of the household ; and sometimes, also, as you watch the school-boys in the play-ground. You will find them on the street and in the store; on the ship and in the railway car; in the field of nature and on the page of literature; in history, biography, science, art ; in a word, everywhere.

Some one has said that " Learning to paint is learning to see ; " so I would say, " Learning to illustrate is learning to see." The preacher who compels himself for a time to look at everything with the question in his mind, " What use can I make of this in commending the truth of God to my fellow-men ? " will by and by discover that he has been prosecuting these researches unconsciously. It will become the habit of his life to carry them on. Every journey that he takes he will bring home with him new treasures. Every visit that he pays to the work-shop of the mechanic, the studio of the artist, or the laboratory of the man of science, will give him new spoils. Nay, after the faculty has been fairly cultivated, it will lay hold of his past accumulations and make them fertile in the freshest analogies. The stories he heard in his boyhood; the scenes and circumstances of his youth; the characters he met with in his native town, as well as the old brown-backed books which long ago he read ere yet he had left his father's house; all will be laid under tribute, and will be found rich in materials for this valuable purpose.

As the poet, under Wordsworth's tuition, finds poetry everywhere, so the preacher, under the inspiration of the Lord himself, will find illustrations anywhere. Dr. John Ker, in his pleasant reminiscences of Guthrie at his Highland home in Vacation-time,* tells us that he saw in the landscape of Inchgrundle the originals of many of his most striking similes; and many a harvest of the same sort has Mr. Beecher reaped from the fields of his Peekskill farm.

Nay, He whom we all alike call Master and Lord, found all nature, and every phasis of human life, suggestive of spiritual truths. The hen with her brood under her wings and the sparrow chirping on the housetop; the lily in its snowy loveliness and the mustard tree in its growth from a tiny seed; the

---

* "Guthrie's Autobiography and Memoir," ut sup.: Vol. II., pp. 348–360.

housewife kneading her dough, or sweeping her room in eager search after the piece of money which she had lost; the sower going forth to sow; and the vine-dresser with his pruning-hook; all were introduced into His discourses in such a way that each became thenceforth associated in the minds of His hearers with some aspect of divine truth. And this was one of the reasons why, with a Joseph and Nicodemus among His disciples, "the common people," also, "heard Him gladly." For here, in their liking for the illustrative, "the rich and the poor meet together." And both alike will be drawn to the sanctuary by the magnetism of its simplicity.

But it is necessary to give a few cautions as to the use of illustrations. And here, in the first place, let me say, that you should not attempt to illustrate that which is already perfectly plain. Do not hold up a lighted taper under pretence of making the sun visible. The great luminary can shine for himself; he does not require your puny rushlight to make his glory conspicuous. Few things are more ridiculous than to hear a would-be orator laboriously illustrating a truth which is almost axiomatic. When you have such a principle to lay down, state it with emphatic clearness, and pass on. I was once listening to a preacher who was descanting on the certainty of death after this fashion: "As sure as to-morrow's sun will rise, as sure as the tidal wave keeps its appointed time, and as sure as"—a great many other things, when a friend who was sitting beside me gave utterance to these words, which, for me, at least, blew the preacher's rhetoric into atoms, " Tut ! tut ! what does he mean ? Do not the very boys on the street seal their bargains with the phrase, ' As sure's death ? ' Can't he say that and press forward ? " What is already clear can only be dimmed by the attempt to illustrate it. You cannot handle crystal without leaving on it the marks of your touch, and they mar its transparency. Therefore, when you are dealing with anything which is perfectly plain in itself, leave it " simplex munditiis," for such truths " when unadorned " are " adorned the most."

Again, do not use too many illustrations for the same purpose. The effect of this prodigality will be to dazzle your hearers, and you will leave them bewildered, when, perhaps, you think you have succeeded in leading them to a clear apprehension of your point. In a display of fireworks, the last series of dissolving showers of variegated sparks puts all that went before it out of mind, and very soon it, too, will fade from the spectator's memory, leaving only a vague impression of something magnificent. So, in a string of illustrations, one will jostle another out of the hearer's mind, and he will go away with a wonderful idea of the wealth of your resources, but with a very slight impression of the importance of the truth which you have been attempting to enforce. Remember that everything you say is virtually thrown away by you if it do not bear on the elucidation or application of that subject to which your discourse is professedly devoted. You are not to empty out your commonplace book before the eyes of your people that they may marvel at your industry in collecting so much, but you are to make the truth plain to them, even if they should never think of you.

I once spent an evening with an enthusiastic microscopist, and I observed that always before he asked me to look through his instrument, he adjusted a focal mirror in such a way as to bring a bright point of light to bear upon the object on the glass, and then when I looked in I saw the butterfly's wing, or whatever it might be, not only magnified, but illumined. Now, one illustration which, like that mirror, will focalize the light of analogy upon your theme, will be worth a score of second-rate similitudes which merely momentarily flicker before it. One lamp is worth a million fire-flies.

Still, again, do not employ as illustrations things which are recondite and obscure, needing first to be explained themselves. The more simple and familiar your analogies are the better. You are to use that with which your people are already acquainted for the purpose of making clearer to them that which is obscure. Do not turn the sanctuary into a place for the teaching of botany, chemistry, electricity, astronomy, or some other science, in order that you may employ the facts of these departments to illustrate some spiritual truth. Take the great outstanding things which are patent to all, and then the effect will be felt by all; but if you follow the other plan, your discourses will drive away the unlettered with out proving attractive even to the votaries of science.

The editor of the *Preacher's Lantern* tells of a Scotchman who forsook the ministrations of the late James Hamilton for those of a preacher of quite another stamp, and who gave his reasons for the change in these words : " Eh, sir! the doctor is jist a gran' man, but I got tired o' his natural history. A little while ago he took up wi' spiders. I never kent before that there was a science of spiders; what he ca'd arachnology. Well, sir, for a number of Sundays he was always saying something about thae spiders. He was a gran' man, but I couldna get on with his natural history."* The author of " Life in Earnest " had many other store-houses of illustration than that of science, and made full proof of his ministry in the scattering of similitudes of every sort all along his pathway, but such an incident, even in his career, may well serve as a caution to meaner men.

You will misunderstand me, however, if you suppose that I would debar you from the employment of any analogy which scientific research may suggest. On the contrary, some of these are so simple in themselves, and so striking when wisely applied, that you would be doing yourselves a great injustice if you were to refuse their aid. Only study variety in your employment of them. Do not go always to the same quarter in search of them. Gather them from every field. Be not so constantly referring to the ocean, that men will say that your occupation will be gone when " there shall be no more sea." Have no specialty

---

* " The Preacher's Lantern," Vol. II., p. 21.

in this department, but welcome analogy no matter from what quarter it may come to you.

Do not be afraid even of one which may have a dash of humor in it. I would not choose it for the humor of it, but neither would I reject it on that account, if it were peculiarly pat. There are some, indeed, who think it is wrong to utter a word in the pulpit that might make a smile ripple over an audience. And, indeed, if the production of the smile were the only reason for saying it, I should be disposed to agree with them. But if, in spite of the smile, the illustration will rivet a truth in the mind of the hearer, then I should not hesitate to employ it. There is as little that is harmful in the laugh on such an occasion, as there is that is commendable in the tear which flows at the telling of a pathetic story. To try to provoke either, for its own sake, is always contemptible ; but to use both for the higher purpose of commending the truth to the conscience, is really praiseworthy. I think I can see a twinkle in Paul's eye, as he dictates a reference to the " profitableness " of Onesimus in his letter to Philemon ; and, provided we consecrate it to Christ, and keep it always in proper subordination, we may find a place even for humor in the sphere of illustration.

Farther, when we use a fact in science, or an incident in history, or a story from common life, or a process in some ordinary occupation, we must be sure that we have got it accurately. I was one day trying to illustrate something to my Liverpool people, who were familiar with everything about shipping, by the setting sail of a vessel. I used the word "*shrouds*," as if it had been synonymous with "*sails*," and when I saw the smile, half-compassionate, and half-contemptuous, with which my error was received by my hearers, I mentally resolved that I would never again venture on anything in the way of illustration with which I was not absolutely familiar. The auditors must be acquainted with everything which we use for that purpose, that they may feel its force; but we must be accurate in its statement, that we may retain their confidence, for if they see that we cannot be depended on in their department, they will place no reliance on us in our own.

Finally, we must be always careful to let the full force of the illustration go to illuminate the truth which we are expounding. We must not detain the attention of the people on the picture, but use it for the purpose of irradiating the subject which we have in hand. The foot-lights of the theatre are studiously veiled from the eyes of the spectators, but they throw a lustre on the actor's face. Like them, our illustrations must not draw attention to themselves, but cast all their brightness on the truth. Rivet your nail after you have driven it. Do not allow the application of your analogy to take care of itself, but see to it that it leaves the precise impression that you designed it to produce. In your anxiety to do that, however, beware lest you run your illustration into the ground by drawing your simile out into the minutest details. A single phrase, sometimes even two or three words may do the work more effectively than it could be performed in a whole sentence or para-graph. In his famous inaugural address to the stu-dents of the Glasgow University, Brougham, following in the wake of Longinus, directs attention to the excellence of Demosthenes in this respect. He re-minds us that when that ancient orator "would com-pare the effects of the Theban treaty in dispelling dangers that compassed the state round about, to the swift passing away of a stormy cloud, he satisfied himself with the words ὥσπερ νέρος—the just theme of admiration to succeeding ages; and when he would paint the sudden approach of overwhelming peril to beset the state, he does it by a stroke, the picturesque effect of which has not, perhaps, been enough noted, likening it to a whirlwind, or a winter torrent, ὥσπερ σκηπτὸς ἢ χειμάῤῥους." The same authority contrasts these with the weakening amplifications with which Burke marred the effect of his fine description of those who suffered from Hyder's devastations, as "enveloped in a whirlwind of cavalry." The tempta-tion, when one has a good illustration, is to overdo it; and so to overlay that which we are seeking to make plain.

That was the tendency of Dr. Guthrie, and in this regard, his friend, William Arnot, is a much safer model. That which Guthrie would have spread over an entire page, elaborating every particular with pre-Raphael-like minuteness, Arnot would have given in a sentence; and, while the hearer of the former would have said, "What a beautiful illustration!" that of the latter would have exclaimed, "How clear he made it all by that simple figure!"

In the light-house at Sandy Hook, by a beautiful combination of the catoptric and dioptric principles, a reflector behind, and a many-ringed lantern in front, things are arranged in such a manner that no ray from the lamps is lost, but all are bent out to the wide ocean, to bid the mariner welcome to our shores. So in using our illustrations we should contrive to bring every part of them to bear on the truth which is before us. We must not turn them on our own faces; neither must we give our hearers the idea that they have been enjoying an intellectual or oratorical treat, rather than listening to a sermon. Jesus and His truth must be always in the midst, and not only in the midst, but conspicuously there, as the grand themes of our glory and our joy. Macaulay tells us in his brilliant article on Southey's "Bunyan," * that James the Second sat for his portrait to Varelst, the famous flower painter. When the performance was finished, his Majesty appeared in the midst of a bower of sun-flowers and tulips, which completely drew away attention from the central figure, so that all who looked at it took it for a flower piece. Let not the lesson be lost on us. It is as criminal to hide the Christ beneath gorgeous illustrations as it is to ignore Him altogether. He must be supreme. *We* may, and ought, to cover *our* faces before Him; but we must never put a veil, no matter how exquisite may be its texture, over His benignant countenance.

* Macaulay's Critical and Historical Essays. People's edition. Vol. I., p. 133.

LECTURE IX.

THE CONDUCT OF PUBLIC WORSHIP—READING OF
THE SCRIPTURES.

LECTURE IX.

THE CONDUCT OF PUBLIC WORSHIP—READING OF THE SCRIPTURES.

IT may seem strange, at first sight, that in a course of lectures on preaching any place should be found for remark on the devotional services of the sanctuary. But the two things are not generically different. It is alleged, indeed, by many that we who have no formal liturgy, exalt the sermon at the expense of the worship. But they who speak in such a fashion, forget that preaching and hearing from the Word of God, when they are engaged in by pastor and people out of love to Christ, and with a desire to honor Him, are as really worship as praise and prayer. Cornelius was as truly rendering homage to Jehovah, when he said to Peter: " Now, therefore, are we all here present before God to hear all things that are commanded thee of God,"* as when he was on his knees in prayer. And if our modern church-goers were to reflect that still God prepares preacher and hearer for meeting each other, and by the providence of His Spirit gives the one a message for the other, there would be in them both a devouter sense of

---

* Acts x. 33

reverence toward God in the exercises of delivering and listening to a sermon.

Not now, indeed, by " visions on the housetop," does God fit His servants for speaking to their fellow-men, but through the discipline and suggestions of the week; through family cares or pastoral experiences; through public events or private conflicts, He leads them to such a choice of subjects and such a treatment of them, that they have a message specially adapted to at least some of their hearers. And in the same way He has been preparing the hearers for its reception; the ploughshare has made the soil ready for the taking in of the seed. So every sermon that is prepared as in the sight of the Lord finds the Cornelius for whom it was designed; and every Cornelius who comes into the sanctuary seeking to know what is commanded him of God, gets the message for which he was looking. And what is that, if it be not worship? The preaching is regarded by both as an ordinance of God, and so the souls of both are seeking to serve God through it.

But, to look at the matter in another light, every one must perceive that the sermon and the service act and react upon each other. The preacher who begins his discourse after a fervent prayer and an inspiring hymn, is always more animated and earnest than he would have been if the devotional exercises had been languid and formal. And after an impressive sermon, even the most careless worshiper must have been moved by the hush of reverence with which the people join in prayer, and the enthusiasm of soul and voice with which they sing the closing hymn.

Besides, in our form of worship, the main responsibility for the service rests upon the preacher; and so, it cannot be out of place to consider the subject here.

It will not be expected, however, that I should enter into a disquisition upon the general question of worship, or seek to compare the advantages and disadvantages of the different forms which have been adopted by different churches. I am not here to speak of the spectacular ritual of the Church of Rome, or of the liturgical service of the Protestant Episcopalians; neither am I required to insist upon the superiority of our own severely simple form. Each has its own elements of attractiveness; and though, on what we consider Scriptural grounds, we may prefer our own, we may have something better to do than to anathematize the others. The essential things in all worship are that it be spiritual and true; and if we condemn some for exalting certain accessories into indispensable elements of religious service, we must ourselves beware of insisting on the absence of these, as if that were absolutely needful to insure spirituality. Whenever any form or the exclusion of any form is made imperative, there is a danger of imperilling the spirit. That which is worshiped, if it be not God, is an idol, whether it be made merely of lead, or of the purest gold; and if we make an idol of our plain Puritan service, it will be a snare to us, just as really as his processional pomp may be to the High-Church Episcopalian.

But the question with which I have now to deal is this, How shall we conduct that service which is generally adopted among us, so as to secure that it shall be most acceptable to God, and most refreshing and stimulating to us and to the congregation?

Now, here, it is pertinent to remind you that the first grand indispensable qualification for the leading of public devotion is a *filial heart.* The "true worshiper" is he that "worships the Father."* Sonship will attune the heart to spirituality. It is not without great significance, in this regard, that the prayer, so simple in its terms and so wide in its comprehensiveness, which Jesus taught His disciples, should begin with these words, "*Our Father.*" Thus, the Saviour would bid us pause a moment on the very threshold of our devotions, that we may set definitely before our minds what God is to us, ere we go forward to present our petitions. Well has the good Leighton said here: "This is one great cause of our wandering, that we do not, at our entrance into prayer, compose ourselves to due thoughts of God and to set ourselves in His presence; this would do much to ballast our minds, that they tumble not to and fro, as is their custom."† Even if He stood in a less endearing relationship to us, it would still be proper for us, when we pray unto Him, to put clearly before our minds what He is to us and what we are to Him; but since He has revealed Himself in Christ

---

* John iv. 23.

† The Works of Archbishop Leighton, Nelson's Edition, p. 452.

as "Our Father," it is of the highest moment, if our supplications are to be either natural or sincere, that we realize all that such a declaration implies. If, for example, we lose consciousness of His Father-hood, and think of Him only as the Judge who shall render unto every man according to his works, we shall come to the throne of grace as if it were the throne of judgment, and fear and trembling will get hold upon us. If, again, we allow the thought that He is a King to take exclusive possession of our souls, our minds will be so occupied about the manner of our coming to Him that we shall be apt to forget the matter for which we come; and our services may be a pompous ritual, like the ceremonials connected with the court of an earthly prince, but they will be like these also, in a large degree, mere empty forms.

I am persuaded, therefore, that much of the life-lessness and artificialness of our public devotions is to be traced to the fact, that we have not received " the spirit of adoption." The spirit of adoption and the spirit of supplication is one. What liberty is that which a son enjoys? How he comes bounding into our room, no matter how we may be engaged, calcu-lating that we will welcome him, and knowing that when he has laid hold of our fatherhood, he has laid hold of our strength ! How little is there of the artificial or insincere in such an approach as he makes to us ! But it is not otherwise in our applications to God. It is easy to be sincere in offering all the peti-tions of the Lord's Prayer, when we have been able to appropriate the first two words and to call God

"Our Father," and all unnatural and unreal formalism will disappear when we enter fully into the enjoyment "of the glorious liberty of the children of God."

Then, as regards praise, the same thing holds good. What joy a daughter has in singing to her father! There is no thought of weariness or of indifference, but every effort is put forth to please him. So, if we but recognize that God is our Father, and that He is listening to our songs, our hymns will be no longer vapid and uninteresting, but will become heart-stirring and ennobling, and we shall rival David when he says, "My heart is fixed, O God, my heart is fixed! I will sing and give praise. Awake, psaltery and harp, I myself will awake early!"*

Here is the radical cure for dull devotion, powerless prayer, and uninteresting worship. We need no splendid liturgy or gorgeous ritual. We need only a fresh baptism with "the spirit of adoption;" we need only the hearts of sons glowing with love for our God and Father in Christ Jesus, and then, filial happiness filling our souls, "hosannas" will no longer "languish on our tongues," nor prayer come faltering feebly from our lips. The first song of "the morning stars" was accompanied with the joyful shouting of "the sons of God;" and when the worshipers in our modern sanctuaries shall realize their divine relationship, their praises will be but the undertone of the angelic harmonies.

But, bearing in mind this important principle, let

---

* Psalm lvii. 7, 8.

us proceed to take up each of the departments of the public service and see what is needed, in order to give to each its best expression and to get from each the fullest benefit.

I begin with the reading of the Word of God. The day has gone, I trust forever, when the public reading of the Scriptures can be regarded as a work of supererogation, or as a device of a poorly-prepared preacher for filling out the time allotted for the services of the sanctuary. They tell in Scotland that when a worthy minister in Aberdeenshire was remonstrated with by a committee of his parishioners for making this exercise a prominent part of public worship, he covered his censors with confusion by turning to the title-page of the Bible, which, as you know, is printed in Great Britain by royal authority, and showing them these words, " By His Majesty's special command appointed to be read in churches!" But we have " another King, one Jesus," and when we learn that " He went into the synagogue on the Sabbath-day and stood up for to read,"* we have the highest possible warrant for bringing into the foremost place in the exercises of the sanctuary the Word of the living God. It is true, indeed, that the Bible is widely diffused among the people, and that, happily, there is now no longer a " famine of hearing the words of the Lord,"† like that which, in the days of the Reformation in England, made the people throng around the learned clerk as he read out of the great

---

* Luke iv. 16. † Amos viii. 11.

Bible that was chained to the pillar in the crypt of old St. Paul's. But still it is right that the book should be publicly read, not only that all may see that preacher and hearer make it the ultimate standard of appeal, but also that the minds and hearts of the worshipers may be rightly affected as they draw near to God. Besides, one is more deeply moved by what he hears from the lips of another, than by what he reads in his closet. Few portions of the New Testament are more familiar than the eighth chapter of the Romans, and yet, if I may judge from my own experience, much as I always enjoy the perusal of that section of Scripture by myself, I have never heard it read by another without receiving a profounder impression of some part of the argument, or obtaining a fresh glimpse into the meaning of some of its verses. We ought not, therefore, to regard this part of the service as of subordinate importance, or to engage in it in a perfunctory manner. Let us feel that we are dealing with the Word of God, and that will produce within us such reverence and docility of spirit, that as we read, the people will be hushed into attentiveness, and will listen, not as unto us, but as unto God. If we go into it as a mere form, or because it is a part of what are commonly, but very erroneously, called, the introductory services, we shall read automatically, having ourselves no intelligent apprehension of the meaning of what we read, and giving no help or light to those who hear. But, if in our own sanctified imagination we place ourselves before the God and Father of our Lord Jesus Christ, and hear

Him speaking to ourselves, we shall succeed in interpreting Him to the people, so that they will listen and obey. The first canon here, therefore, as in all else, is that you be yourselves really impressed with what you read.

A few hints, however, may be added from one's own experience. Be sure, then, in the first place, that the passage which you select is adapted for public reading. " All Scripture is given by inspiration of God, and is profitable ;" but it is not all equally well-fitted for public perusal. Some two or three years ago, an intimate friend from the other side of the Atlantic, occupied my pulpit, and read the latter half of the third chapter of Luke's gospel, which consists of the genealogy of Joseph, the reputed father of Jesus, and as he went on with the ever-recurring phrase, " which was the son of," " which was the son of," " which was the son of," etc., I saw a broad grin spreading over the faces of the people, which indicated that he had made a great mistake. When he announced his text in the words, " Adam, which was the son of God," I could see why he had chosen to read such a passage ; but still the fact that his theme was taken from the last entry in the table, was no proper reason for reading the whole of it, and the amusement of his hearers at the strangeness of his selection, was a most unfortunate preparation, or rather it was an actual disturbance of their minds for the prayer which followed.

Choose your passages for reading from your knowledge of the circumstances of your people, as well as out of regard to the topic which you are about to submit to their consideration. It is well, as far as possible, to give unity to the service; yet that must not be sought at the sacrifice of any important interest. The didactic ought to yield to the devotional, rather than the devotional to the didactic; and if you cannot find some portion of Scripture which shows the devotional bearing of the subject which you are going to treat, then make your selection on the general principle of securing that which will be most appropriate to the greatest number of your parishioners. Your pastoral visitation, of which I shall have more to say in another Lecture, will be of great assistance to you here; for your knowledge of the characters and conditions of your people which you acquire thereby, will enable you to fix upon such portions of Scripture as will be truly helpful to them, and to present such petitions as will carry up with them the burdens of their hearts to God. That which you select with one case in view will commonly meet many others, and not seldom a hearer may take you by the hand and thank you for throwing a new light on his path, by directing his attention to a passage which he had never noted before, but which he now feels to be unspeakably precious to him.

You will find a rich treasury of such sustaining sayings in the book of Psalms, and a precious storehouse of them in the four gospels, while the experience of the apostles, as unfolded in their epistles, can scarcely ever be inappropriate. But your own private devotional reading will be here your greatest helper, for what you have found to be profitable to your own soul, will always be serviceable to others, especially because in your reading of that there will be such emphasis of emotion unconsciously made, as shall infallibly arrest the attention of the hearer, and reveal to him the peculiar shade of thought which has so affected you.

While, however, in the public reading of the Scriptures it is well to give particular prominence to the devotional portions of the Word of God, you must not overlook the practical or the doctrinal. Religion is a creed and a life as well as an emotion, and in order that it should be the last in any real and rational sense, it must also be the former two. This is probably the reason why in the liturgy of the Episcopal Church a place has been made for the recitation of the creed and for the reading of the ten commandments, as well as for the use of the litany. Now we may act upon this same principle while yet we do not confine ourselves to the use of these forms. Thus at one time we may give prominence to the doctrine of the Incarnation, by using the first portion of the Gospel by John; and at another we may set clearly forth the doctrine of the atonement, by reading the third chapter of the Romans. Similarly we may place distinctly before the minds of the hearers the work of the Holy Ghost in regeneration, by the selection of the third chapter of John's gospel; or the blessedness of the forgiveness of sins by choosing the 32d psalm.

Again, we may find a place on one day for the reading of the law; on another for the Sermon on the Mount; on another, for some portion from the Epistle of James; and on yet another, for one of the concluding chapters of the Epistle to the Romans.

Thus, that which has been done for Episcopalians by the compilers of the Prayer-Book, in their observance of the festivals of the Christian year, we may and ought to do for ourselves. We should not leave our selection of passages to the mood of the moment, or the hap-hazard of the morning, but should endeavor to observe some system in accordance with which we shall be able to give its proper place to each of the various departments of " doctrine, reproof, correction, and instruction in righteousness." For this purpose all parts of the sacred volume should be laid under tribute, and you will do well to pay especial attention to those unfrequented portions of it, in which will be found some of its most startling utterances, and some of its most beautiful and consoling sayings. At any rate, have some plan which you follow, so that at length your readings shall give a full-orbed presentation of Christian truth.

Then, as to the length of your selections, you must be guided by circumstances. The division into chapters, though very convenient for many purposes, is not always happily made, and may occasionally be disregarded. Sometimes it may be well to read more than one chapter, and sometimes a brief section may suffice. Only do not let it be too brief. Many pastors, as it seems to me, deal with the Scriptures homeopathically, and give them out in globules and triturations. They seem to be afraid to read more than a very few verses, and judging from their manner all through, you would infer that it was a weariness to read even so few. They are impatient to be at their sermon, or they know that they have a somewhat longer discourse than usual, and the Bible reading must make way for their lucubrations. Now, that is all wrong. Read such a portion, as that all who hear you may understand that you regard God's Word as of prime importance. Why should we not occasionally take even so large a section as the entire Sermon on the Mount? or a whole division of Paul's argument in the Epistle to the Romans? Well read, I can conceive that such passages would have tremendous power, while the unity of design running through them, would certainly have an effect on the understanding as well as on the hearts of the hearers.

Give your whole attention to that which you are reading. Forget your sermon for the time. Dismiss, meanwhile, from your mind all thought about the prayer which you are about to offer. Let your whole soul be concentrated on the portion of God's Word which you have selected, else your reading will be lifeless and perfunctory. I have heard a distinguished clergyman say that frequently his mind was so preoccupied with the discourse which he was about to deliver, that his reading of the Scriptures was mechanical, and when it was over he could not have told what the chapter was about. Now, it is impossible that any one should interest his people in the Word of God, if he reads it publicly in such a fashion as that. Remember that it is God's word you are dealing with, and that greater results may be expected from that than from any preaching of yours. The reading ought not to be subordinate to your sermon, but your sermon ought to be subordinate to it. Indeed, the end of your preaching will be secured, in a large measure, when you have stirred up the hearers to search the Scriptures, whether the things which you have spoken are confirmed by them or not; but if, in your public treatment of the Word of God, you are listless and mechanical, you cannot hope to interest any one in the study of it. The eloquent McAll, of Manchester, England, is reported to have said : " If the Lord had appointed two officers in His Church, the one to preach the Gospel and the other to read the Scriptures, and had given me the choice of these, I should have chosen to be a reader of the inspired Word of God," and with such an opinion, we are not surprised to learn that he excelled in that exercise ; nay, it is not improbable that his deep reverence for the Bible so manifested, contributed largely to the power of his discourses.

Endeavor to indicate the meaning of the passage by your mode of reading it. Good reading is good interpretation ; and delicate shades of significance which you have discovered for yourself in the study, may be revealed by your emphasis even without a word of explanation. Examples in illustration of this assertion will readily occur to you. Thus in the chapter on the resurrection of the dead, in the first Epistle to the Corinthians, most people read the

words, " For this corruptible must put on incorruption," as if the word "must" were simply the auxiliary
to the verb "put on;" but in the original we find that
the phrase literally means, "For it is necessary that
this corruptible should put on incorruption," and so
good reading will make the "must" emphatic; and
when that is done, it is seen at once that the verse has
an important part in the apostle's argument.

Again, in the first verse of John's gospel, the full
force of the words is lost in the reading which is common, and which puts the emphasis on "was," but
when we enter fully into the meaning of the Evangelist and lay the stress on the several predicates instead of on the copula, thus—" In the beginning was
the *word;* and the word was WITH GOD; and the word
was GOD;" then the force of the verse as an assertion
of the Deity of the Word is overwhelming.

So in Paul's injunction to the Romans, "If it be
possible, as much as lieth in you, live peaceably with
all men," the point is lost by emphasizing the "in,"
as is so commonly done, for that makes the second
clause only a reduplication of the first; but when we
put the stress on "you," and read thus, "If it be possible, as much as lieth in *you*, live peaceably with all
men," the hearer is at once reminded that though he
is not responsible for the obstacles to peace existing
in other people, he is accountable for all that are in
himself, and he is exhorted to see to it, that if there
shall be any divisions, the causes of them shall be in
others and not in him.

Again, how often is the sense of the Saviour's

words about the salt weakened by a false emphasis! Most people put the "it" into the shade, thus, "If the salt have lost its savor, wherewith shall it be salted?" But when the "it" is made emphatic, the question is immediately suggested, "How shall the savorless salt be salted?" and the fearful condition of a Christless Church is vividly set before the imagination of the hearer.

In the same way, by a delicate intonation, the pride and sullenness of the elder brother may be thus brought out, "Lo! these many years do *I* serve thee, neither transgressed *I* at any time thy commandment, and yet thou never gavest *me* a kid, that I might make merry with my friends; but as soon as this *thy son* was come, which hath devoured thy living with harlots, thou hast killed for *him* the fatted calf." And the sharpness of the arrow aimed by Jesus at the heart of the woman of Samaria will be felt when we read His words thus: "Thou hast well said, I have no husband, for thou hast had five husbands, and he whom thou now hast is not thy *husband*:* in that saidst thou truly."

These may seem to you very little things, but, as Michael Angelo once said, "they contribute to perfection, and that is not a little thing." Besides, their apparent minuteness, coupled with the undoubted light which attention to them sheds upon the several

---

* In the original the σου is found, and it is just possible the emphasis may be on "thy," indicating that the man was some one else's husband; but as ἄνδρα is throughout emphatic, I prefer the reading which I have given in the text.

passages, suggests the inference that great attention should be given to preparation for the public reading of the Scriptures. You ought to study the passage carefully beforehand, if possible, with the original at your side, and you should, by the help of every exegetical appliance at your command, make up your mind as to the meaning which it bears, so that you may indicate that perfectly to those who hear you. Do not delude yourself into the belief that it is an easy thing to read thus. In truth, there are few things so hard, and it has come to be much harder than otherwise it might have been, because preachers generally persist in thinking that it is easy. For myself, I should be disposed to test a man's pulpit efficiency by his reading of the Scriptures, fully more than by any other of the public exercises, for it will reveal at once whether he is a reverent student of the Bible ; whether he is a careful exegete ; and whether he is a man of thoroughness, carrying his principle and preparation into everything. Because men usually make this matter of so little account, it is a case for the application of the Saviour's words, " He that is faithful in that which is least, is faithful also in much ; and he that is unjust in the least, is unjust also in much." When I hear good reading of the Scriptures, I expect to find that the man is also attentive to all the details of the ministry, and I am rarely disappointed.

Do not take it for granted, therefore, that you can read well enough ; or that you are competent to give effective utterance to any passage *ad aperturam libri.*

Extempore preaching may do for some, but extempore reading is impossible for anybody. Of course it is easy to name the words correctly, but that is not reading. That is only accelerated spelling. Reading is the presentation through the voice of the thoughts which the sacred author has put into words: and for that, study is indispensable. You might as well expect an actor to give a perfect presentation of a character, on his first reading of a play, as imagine that a preacher can, without previous preparation, give a proper rendering of any passage in any author, how much less in a book so many-sided and suggestive as the Bible. Always prepare yourself for this exercise, therefore, and at length your reading of the Scriptures may be as effective in the conversion of sinners, and the edification of the people of God, as any sermon.

But the question is often asked, Ought the reader to indulge in running comments? In answer, we have to say, that in such a matter, very much will depend upon the qualifications of the minister and on the character of his congregation. Many men have what one may call a happy knack of saying suggestive things, in course of their reading of the Scriptures, which amounts almost to genius. It is impossible to listen to the incidental remarks of Mr. Spurgeon or Dr. Cumming on the morning lesson, without both admiration and edification. But their eminence in this particular department has called into existence a host of imitators, whose success, to say the least, is not encouraging to others. They aim at saying what is striking, and they end in uttering some pompous platitude, or some ridiculous absurdity. In their efforts to barb the arrow, they only blunt it ; and under the guise of explaining the meaning of the sacred writer, they succeed admirably in taking off the edge of his words. Unless, therefore, you have a peculiar aptitude for saying pithy, motto-like things, which condense a great deal into a very few words, you had better let the running commentary, as it is called, alone.

Perhaps, however, you may be settled over a people who, from their habits or their education, are not able to command their attention for any length of time upon a single subject, and in such a case you may find it profitable to abridge the length of the sermon proper, and make a few telling remarks on the passage which you read. To do that well, you must make as careful preparation for it as for a more formal exposition ; studying attentively not only the original Scriptures, but also everything that the best expositors at your command have said upon the section. A good model for such work is furnished in Mr. Spurgeon's " Treasury of David," which, over and above its value, from its references to the works of others, is beyond all price for the illustration which it gives of the best mode of turning the utterances of David to practical and devotional account. Peculiarly serviceable, also, will be the commentary of Matthew Henry, especially in those places where he says "Note here "— for after such an introduction you may look for some specimen of sanctified wit, or some nugget of heavenly wisdom.

But in making such remarks, do not mix them up indiscriminately with the Word of God. Read the passage distinctly and intelligently, that it may stand clearly before the minds of the people in its own unapproachable sublimity; but beware of interjecting your comments parenthetically in such a fashion that the hearer, unless he is already familiar with the chapter, may not at first be able to distinguish what is yours from what is in the book. Do not indulge in flippancies, which may destroy that sense of reverence which ought ever to be felt when you are handling the Word of God. And if you have no remark of explanation to offer, or no inference of a practical sort to draw, say nothing; for comment is valuable only when it illustrates the obscure, or suggests that which might otherwise have been unthought of. God's Word can speak for itself, and where it is perfectly clear, it will be more forcible without your remarks than with them.

Throughout my ministry in Liverpool I followed the plan of accompanying my reading by an appendix of comment ; and in that way, in the course of sixteen years, beginning at Genesis I had gone over the books of the Old Testament as far as that of Ecclesiastes ; but though it was the means of increasing my own familiarity with the Scriptures, and was acknowledged to be both exceedingly interesting and instructive, especially to the young, yet as the years advanced, it grew less attractive to me, and when I began my labors in New York, I left out this feature of the service. It broke in upon the unity of the exercises as a whole; it amounted sometimes in itself almost to a minor sermon; it tended to protract the morning services to an undue length, and so, when the opportunity of a new pastorate was afforded me, I determined to dispense with it altogether.

So far as my experience goes, therefore, it is not decisive on either side. Here as in other things I would not fetter you with any Medo-Persic laws. Do not make a comment unless it is absolutely irrepressible. But when you have something that you feel you must say, say it, and go on. Encourage your people to have Bibles in their own hands that they may follow you as you proceed. That was perhaps the greatest advantage which resulted from my Liverpool practice. The members of the congregation learned to make the Word of God a subject of study, and came prepared to note what might be said. We read in course, and so the morning lesson was in a great degree like the exercises of a large Bible-class, and proved interesting alike to old and young.

But in America the Bible is a stranger in the pew. What the reason for that is, I cannot discover; yet the effect is bad. It disposes the preacher to take short texts which his hearers may remember even without looking for them in the book. It discourages him from presenting a Biblical argument, or making any large induction of passages for the purpose of coming to a Scriptural conclusion; and especially it puts a great obstacle in the way of expository preaching. I would favor anything which would remedy this great evil. *The Bible must be in the pew, if it is to keep its place in the pulpit.* Wherever you may be settled, make an early request that your people will bring with them their copies of the Word of God; then see you to it, that they make good use of them when they do bring them.

"To the law and to the testimony, if they speak not according to this word, it is because they have no light in them." "Seek ye out of the book of the Lord, and read." "Search the Scriptures." "Give attendance to reading." These are the commands of Him who gave the book, and everything which will stimulate to their obedience is to be welcomed and encouraged.

In a Scottish congregation few sounds are more inspiring to the preacher than the rustle of the leaves of hundreds of Bibles, as he bids his hearers turn with him to a passage which has an important bearing on his argument, and the corner pressed down, as he finishes his remarks, indicates that the owner of the book means to study it in the leisure of his closet. When you can get your people to use the Word of God in that way, both in the sanctuary and the home, as the testimony to regulate their faith and the law to rule their lives, your ministry will be a success. And, if you be wise, you will endeavor so to shape your public reading of it, that whether with comment, or without, it may, with your discourse, contribute to the formation and fostering of such a habit.

LECTURE X.

THE CONDUCT OF PUBLIC WORSHIP—PRAISE AND
PRAYER.

LECTURE X.

THE subject of public praise is so environed with
controversies, that one cannot reach it without
passing through them. But a few firm steps will
carry us safely over all burning questions, and the
more quickly we take them, we shall be the less in-
jured by the flames.

Some insist that we shall confine ourselves in this
exercise to the use of inspired productions; yet, in
the matter of prayer, which is the nearest of kin to
praise, they have no objections to join with a brother
who is employing extempore language; while in the
metrical versions of the psalms which they sing, there
is very frequently a marring of the original grandeur
of the odes by the imperfections, and even errors of
the rhymer. So, while repudiating merely human
utterances, they are compelled to accept them after all.

Others have conscientious objections to the employment of instrumental music in the leading of
"the service of song in the house of the Lord;" but
while we must ever respect a conviction which is
maintained from the determination to be true to God,
it does not seem to have struck the friends who hold
this view, that to be consistent, they ought to discard

the use of the music-book and of set tunes, as well as
that of the organ.   In the music-book the notes are
in symbol, and address themselves to the eyes of the
initiated; by the organ the notes are produced in
sound, and address themselves to the ears of all.
Thus there is no difference in principle between the
two, while, as appealing more powerfully to the
people as a whole, and giving them a greater degree
of assistance, the advantage is unquestionably on the
side of the instrument.

Moreover, in the employment of a precentor, the
friends who have these conscientious scruples are
hiring an organ.   No doubt the man may be a good,
godly Christian, but he is not engaged by the church
because of that; he is employed because he has an
organ, and can play well upon it; and if his organ
gets out of repair—in other words, if he loses his voice
—he is dispensed with, and another is employed in his
stead.   So the logical result of the argument is, that
if it is wrong to use an organ, then neither set tunes
nor a precentor should be tolerated, and each worshiper should be encouraged to " make a joyful
noise " at his own sweet will.

It is true, indeed, that the larynx is an instrument
made by God, while the organ is a human contrivance;
but if it be wrong to employ the latter for the assistance of the former in singing a hymn, then it must be
equally wrong to avail one's self of the human contrivance of spectacles for the help of the divinely-
constructed organ of the eye in reading it.   So, if
the question were one of argument alone, it is easy

to reduce the whole of these objections to absurdities.

Others still are decidedly opposed to the employment of choirs who shall sing, at stated times, apart from the congregation. They say that singing is simply and only the expression of the soul's emotions unto God, and that it is never to be employed for the purpose of producing an impression on the heart of the worshiper. But, in the consciousness of every one who joins in the exercise of praise, there is undeniably a very strong reflex effect produced, and if that be so, it can hardly be doubted that it was a part of the design of God in encouraging His people to offer praise, that such an effect should be produced. When Luther sung " Ein feste burg," he was inspirited thereby for conflict, and they are the noblest heroes in the battle of life, who enter on it, and maintain it to the music of a psalm. Now the reflex influence being proper enough in itself, may occasionally be made the direct object, and it is that which, in theory at least, churches seek to do through the agency of the choir.

The singing of the Gospel, as in the case of Mr. Sankey, may be as much blessed to the saving of men's souls as the preaching of it ; nay, as the saintly Herbert has said :

> " A verse may catch him who a sermon flies,
> And turn delight into a sacrifice."

All that is needed is that the members of the choir should be themselves in sympathy with the message which they sing, and that they should seek, as relig-

iously as the minister in the pulpit, to forget themselves, and give up all effort at display, in the absorbing desire to glorify Christ.   Given a choir of that
saintly sort, and the singing of its members will be a
joy to the minister and a blessing to the church.
But if the singers be musicians and nothing more—men
and women who are anxious only to let it be heard
how they can perform—then their presence will be an
intrusion in the sanctuary, and their influence will
damp all enthusiasm, and chill every ardent feeling,
alike in the preacher and his people.

In themselves all these matters are of little moment.   They become of importance only as they are
pushed unduly into prominence.   They are not worth
a quarrel or a controversy.   Therefore, when you settle as a pastor over any church, do not attempt rashly
to alter any existing order of things in musical matters.   Accept the situation and make the very best
of it for the glory of God and the edification of the
people.   "Art thou called" to a church without an
organ, "care not for it;" but if thou mayest obtain
one, "use it rather."   Only remember this, that nothing will more interfere with your usefulness or mar
your happiness, than the stirring up of a musical controversy.   Let well alone.   The best all round is very
often lost by attempting to have the absolute best in
any one department.   In the organ itself, if every
note be separately tuned up to the scale, discord will
be the effect when one attempts to play upon it, for,
as it is an imperfect instrument, most of the fifths
must be left somewhat flat and the few others made

somewhat sharp, the octaves alone being put in perfect unison. So, if we attempt to bring the music
in the church up to that point of perfection which we
think it ought to reach, we shall most likely put the
whole church out of tune. We must make the best
of things as a whole, and be content sometimes with
a little less in one department in order that we may
have harmony in all.* Peace in a church is essential
to progress. The dew is not shed forth in storm, but
in the gentle calm of the Summer's eve it distils on
every blade of grass. So the Spirit comes not down
amid controversy and debate, but where brethren are
"dwelling together in unity," there "the Lord com-
mandeth the blessing, even life for evermore." No organ that was ever built, no choir that ever sang, is for a
moment to be preferred to those higher matters of
spiritual life, for the fostering of which the Church
of Christ exists. "The life is more than meat, and
the body than raiment." The church is more
than music, and it is the most arrant folly for either
minister or music committee to imperil the welfare of
souls for a mere question of taste. A church in regard to all such matters should be like Wordsworth's

---

* Let me direct attention here to Mrs. Alfred Gatty's very pertinent little story, entitled "Imperfect Instruments," contained
in the fourth series of her beautiful "Parables from Nature." I
am indebted to it for the illustration taken from the organ in the
text, but the story itself is one of the most wholesome and suggestive Lectures on Pastoral Theology which I have ever read.

cloud, "which moveth all together when it moves at
all." So if you desire any change, wait till you can
carry the great body of the people along with you,
and meanwhile make the best of what you have.

But now, as to the fostering of congrega'ional praise.
Let me suppose that you are the pastor of a church,
in which, as in the Broadway Tabernacle, the com-
promise exists that the members of the choir sing by
themselves a chant and an anthem, while at each service
two hymns are sung by the congregation. Practically
in such a case, you will have little to say in the selection of the anthems, and yet, if you care to keep
yourself *en rapport* with the leader and the members
of the choir, your influence will be felt, even when
you do not seem to be exerting it. And you ought
to care to keep yourself thus in sympathy with them.
If you regard them as hirelings merely—that will
lead to the manifestation by them of the hireling
spirit. But if you have a frank and generous conference with them on the subject of praise ; if you give
them to understand that you look upon them as your
fellow-laborers, and that you desire to have them always in unison with you ; above all, if you indicate to
them that you wish them to sing for the glory and
in the service of Christ ; then, from my own experience, I am warranted to say, that you may have the
highest happiness in their co-operation, and, even, if
some of them may have been unconverted when they
came to you, the effect of your fellowship on them
may be to lead them to the Lord. If we are to have
choirs at all, then we shall degrade and demoralize

them by speaking of them as "necessary evils," or by giving any countenance to the idea that they and the ministers are "natural enemies." Let it be your earnest endeavor to gain the confidence and secure the affection of the members of your choir, and when you have accomplished that, everything will be easy; for then your advice will be sought with deference, and carried out with thoroughness, when in other circumstances your request would be resisted as dictation. Your power over the choir should be that of influence, rather than authority; for influence moves men and women to yield, while authority will dispose them to resist. A few drops of oil rightly applied, will stop the creaking of a wheel which might jangle the nerves of multitudes; and other people's demeanor toward you is the mirror in which your treatment of them is reflected back upon yourself.

But now in regard to the choice of your hymns. Let your selection be restricted within manageable limits. I have a profound conviction that the great size of our hymn-books is helping to kill our congregational praise. No church is able as a whole multitude to sing equally well such a number of tunes as are needed for the rendering of the thirteen or fifteen hundred hymns of which our popular collections consist. The really good hymns in our language are not more than three hundred, and the first thing you will have to do, will be to make your own smaller hymn-book out of the larger ones now in existence. Mark the tunes that go well in the great congregation, and stick to them as closely as possible. If at any time you give out one that drags, or is left to be sung by the choir alone, put a beacon over it, and never give it out again. Thus in a comparatively short time, you will by a species of "natural selection" have made for yourself a hymn-book within the hymn-book; and without saying a syllable on the subject, you will have developed a wonderful enthusiasm for congregational singing.

Four years ago the singing at the Tabernacle was anything but congregational. Still I made no public remark upon it. I waited patiently for nine months, until a new hymn-book, by the vote of the church, was introduced. Then I proceeded on the principle which I have just described; refusing the most appropriate hymn, if it were set to a tune which the people could not or would not sing, and contenting myself with one whose sentiment was less pertinent to my theme, if only the tune was such as evoked enthusiasm. The result has been, that the Tabernacle singing has been often remarked on by strangers for its heartiness and universality, while by the people themselves it is positively delighted in. There is no need here of repeated exhortation. Nothing is to me more repulsive than the efforts of a minister to "whip up" the singing, by continually entreating the people to exert themselves, or by the impertinent interjection of similar interludes of insistance between the stanzas. The thing is largely in the pastor's own hand, and in the manner which I have sketched he may without a word accomplish all he desires. For the people love to sing; and they will always sing when they can; but when they are asked to join in tunes which have an intricate or disagreeable character, and have "no unison with the Creator's praise," they prefer to be silent. The less you speak about it the better, if you will only wisely provide for its general enjoyment.

Two or three other matters here, minute though they be, require attention. Read the hymns distinctly and appreciatively as you give them out. That which is worth singing well is worth reading well. If you are careless or indifferent about the latter, the people will be so also about the former. Do not name the hymn and sit down, as if you were in haste to get through the entire service. In public worship nothing should seem to be huddled up. "He that believeth shall not make haste." And if you believe that God is in the midst of the people, you will be reverentially calm. Many leap over the reading of the lesson and the announcing of the hymns as if they were riding a steeple-chase, and eager only to get as soon as possible to the benediction. Take time, and by your reading prepare the minds of the people for turning the poetry into praise.

Then rise with the people and sing with them yourself. Do not give them the idea that you regard the praise as only furnishing a breathing-time for you; but give yourself up to the privilege of the moment, and let the hymn carry your heart also up with it to Him to whom it ascends. Let no sexton, or usher, or deacon, or any one else, presume to come up into the pulpit with any announcement, or to make any communication to you during the praise, any more than during the prayer. And if you have a brother with you in the pulpit, do not indulge in conversation with him while the people are singing. Example here is better than precept, and the sight of your interest in the song will lead those who might otherwise have been careless to join in with you. You are a worshiper as well as each of them, and no stronger obligation rests on them than on you to take part in the praise.

Finally remember, that the best praise comes after a living sermon.

A bishop visiting a new church, was asked by some one where he would advise that the stove should be put, and he is reported to have replied : " Tell your rector to put the stove in the pulpit." So one of the chief factors in the production of congregational singing is an enthusiastic preacher.

There is nothing so overpowering to me in the public services of the Sabbath, as the singing of the last hymn. It gathers up into itself the whole inspiration of the occasion, and sends pastor and people forth with the highest and holiest aspirations. If that service of praise drags, you may generally conclude that you have failed in your sermon ; but if it rises into the fervor of a devout enthusiasm and stimulates every one to unite in its strain, *that* is the attestation that the hearers have been benefited, and the prophecy that they will begin to live out what you have been enforcing.

But it is time that we should say something about

public prayer. That is the most difficult as it is the most important part of the exercises of the sanctuary; and in churches like ours, where no formal liturgy is used, it does not always receive the attention which it demands. Every earnest minister will tell you that the prayer gives the tone to the entire service. It is the key of the position. It holds in itself the success or the failure of the day. He who is fervent and believing in his petitions, laying hold of God's strength, will be mighty also with men; while the formal suppliant will be but a feeble preacher.

But more even than the sermon the prayer requires preparation. It needs the culture of the heart. The devotion of the pulpit must have its roots back in the closet. The habit of the life will fill a reservoir from which the exercises of the sanctuary will be easily supplied. Great advantage will be derived from the perusal on the Lord's day morning of some portions of the psalms, or other devotional sections of the Word of God. That will attune the spirit into harmony with the engagements of God's house, and put it into a devotional frame. Attention may be profitably given, also, to the prayers of Paul which are ever and anon welling up in his epistles; while the closet writings of such uninspired authors as Augustine, A'Kempis, Leighton, Tholuck, and others may be studied with great profit.

Combined with this preparation of the heart, there must be a deliberate consideration of the circumstances and necessities of our fellow-worshipers. On the morning of the Sabbath throw yourself back on the experiences of the week. You have been mingling with your people. You have seen the backsliding of some, and the conflict of others; the anguish of the bereaved and the depression of the sick; the sorrow of the heavy-laden and the weariness of those who have " forgotten their resting-place. " You know thus the secrets of many homes into which you have been welcomed as an elder brother; and so the stream of your devotion will flow through them all, and sweep away with it every care, and trial, and distress, carrying all on to the ocean of God's loving-kindness. Thus trust and peace, and a sense of the most delightful relief, will come into the hearts of those whose prayers you are leading, and as they raise their heads they will exclaim, " It is a good thing to draw near to God."

Furthermore, we must have in ourselves an unwavering conviction of the profit of prayer. " He that cometh unto God must believe that He is, and that He is the rewarder of them who diligently seek Him." The promises of God must be clearly before our minds. We must have a sense of security in building our expectations of an answer on the merits and mediation of the Lord Jesus Christ. And all through, we must stir ourselves up to take hold of God.

Now, to attain all these things, we ought to have, immediately before the public services, a season of uninterrupted privacy. It is the habit, in many places, for deacons, or members of committee, or officials of one sort or another, to crowd into the vestry or study for the ten minutes preceding the commencement of the worship, and among them all the mind and the heart of the pastor are distracted by requests concerning notices or other matters equally trivial. This is a serious evil. It springs, for the most part, from the merest thoughtlessness, and a gentle hint lovingly given will commonly be enough to rectify it. But rectified it must be, if your prayers are to have that peacefulness which is born of trust and meditation. Hedge yourself in, therefore, as far as possible from all intrusion, before you enter the pulpit. Take time to look all around your people, to commune with your own heart, and to ponder what special things you have to carry with you to the mercy-seat. You will not go on an errand to a fellow man without pausing a little to consider what and how you are to speak to him. But how much more necessary does that premeditation become, when you are the spokesman of your people before the throne of God? When Peter wanted to raise Tabitha, he put all the mourners out of the upper chamber, that he might gather himself up for the great prayer-effort that was before him. And in the same way we should clear our room of all intruders for some time before the service, that we may brace ourselves for the great spiritual exertion that we are so soon to make. For prayer is exertion. When it is real, it is no child's play. It calls every faculty of the soul into strenuous operation. "It is the joint act of the will and the understanding, impelled by the affections;"* hence it is an exhausting labor; and the more thoroughly we enter into it, the more

---

* Canon Liddon's " Some Elements of Religion," pp. 174, 175.

does it wear upon us. Even when he is making no physical effort that will account for such a result, you will see the beads of perspiration standing on the forehead of the earnest minister as he is engaged in prayer; and he knows nothing, as yet, of the responsibilities of the preacher's office, who has not discovered that the most intense, as well as the most important, of his labors is that of public prayer. Keep yourself up for it, therefore, and let no petty details of parish work come in to steal away your attention and devour your strength. The last ten or fifteen minutes in the vestry should be sacredly and unreservedly your own.

So much has been said by others on the different parts of which public prayer is composed, that I shall not enter at all into the consideration of them, save to remark that, in my judgment, the true place for adoration is in the opening hymn. The ascription of honor and glory to God for what He is and for what He has done, is more fittingly sung than said. I would relegate all that, therefore, to the praise, and find expression for it in some prose chant from the psalms, or some sweet lyric like that of Sir Robert Grant.* But with that exception, I would

---

* It begins with this stanza :

> " O worship the King
>   All glorious above ;
> O gratefully sing
>   His power and His love ;
> Our shield and Defender,
>   The ancient of days,
> Pavilioned in splendor
>   And girded with praise."

seek to find a place for all the parts into which prayer
has been divided, and to give due attention to thanksgiving, confession, petition, and intercession.

In the offering of these several constituent elements of the one sacrifice of prayer, certain general
rules ought to be carefully observed.

In the first place, public prayer should be common,
and not minutely individual. The preacher should
not obtrude his own personal experiences and necessities, and ignore the great general wants of the congregation as a whole. His prayer should not be a
pious soliloquy which he simply permits his people
to overhear. Neither should it be a highly-wrought
rhapsody in which the imagination of the speaker
soars to such a height that the average worshiper
cannot accompany him. He must lead the people to
the throne of grace, and give utterance for them
there to the desires which in them are yearning for
expression.

It is not easy always to strike the happy medium
between a generality so vague as to be almost mean-
ingless, and a minuteness so particular as to be all
but unintelligible to the majority of our fellow-sup-
pliants. But the great outstanding needs of a company of men and women are easily recognizable by
us, and these must not be overlooked in our eagerness to get out of the beaten track and have originality in prayer. How has the track come to be
so beaten ? Simply because so many have been required to take it, and so, if we leave it, it is possible that
we may be left to walk alone. What is needed in your

supplications, is not that you should ask things that nobody else had thought of, but that you should carry up on your words the cares and troubles, the burdens and anxieties that are lying heavy and un-spoken on your people's hearts, and leave them with God.   Nor while you do that, need you be afraid that you are bringing the ordinance into contempt ; for when we are dealing with God, the simple rises into the sublime, and there is nothing in all human litera-ture more elevating and ennobling in its character and influence than that exquisite litany, which in words of tenderness and unadorned beauty gives voice to the common wants of the great congrega-tion.   Let it be your aim, therefore, so to shape your utterances that no one in the congregation may have the feeling that there has been nothing said to which he can add Amen.   The most exquisite things that human tongue can articulate will be out of place in your prayers, if they meet nobody's necessity.   The true eloquence of supplication is its appropriateness, and to have that it must be common.   " O Lord," said a pious lady after a public prayer, in which the leader seemed to go round the world, but to forget the purpose for which the worshipers were assembled, " grant me all that person did not ask."   Let us be warned by such a case against the danger of forget-ting that when in the pulpit we lead the prayers of others we must merge self in the community, and unite in asking those things which we all alike require.

In the second place, the prayers of the sanctuary should be petitionary, and not merely meditative or hortatory. Meditation is not prayer, though it is essential as a preparation for it. Pious reflections, therefore, however much they may be valued by us in the closet, should be kept out of our public prayers. The place for them is in the sermon, which now and then may very profitably take the form of a devotional meditation. Prayer is a direct address to God and any reflex action of the soul as it muses on some phase of its own experience, or moralizes from it, is out of place in such an exercise. But if that be true of meditation, it is still more evidently so of exhortation. Our public prayers ought not to be "oblique sermons," which are really addressed to the people, though nominally uttered to God. Our supplications should ascend perpendicularly; we pervert them altogether when we endeavor to make them effective horizontally. I say not, indeed, that when prayer is sincerely offered in the pulpit, it will not have a beneficial influence on the heart of the worshiper, for the contrary is a matter of too common experience to be denied. But that is an incidental result, and so soon as the production of that becomes the principal aim of the minister his supplications cease to be prayers, and degenerate into very feeble and indirect discourses. Do not put a whole system of theology into your supplications. When a minister whom I knew in Scotland had, under the name of prayer, indulged for ten or fifteen minutes in a doctrinal dissertation, making an old sermon serve in place of petition, a venerable Christian matron was overheard to say as he concluded, "O if he had just asked the

Lord for something!" That story, told to me in an early stage of my pastorate, made a deep impression on my heart, and there are few things now of which I am more intolerant than a lesson in theology given in the guise of a prayer.

Be on your guard, also, against insinuating into your prayers the reproof of some irregularity or immorality of which some one of your hearers has been guilty. That is cowardice and irreverence, but it is not prayer. Remember that when you engage in the exercise of prayer in the pulpit, you are there not to ventilate your personal aversions, or to give indirect expression to your individual grudges and grievances, but to be the mouth-piece of the desires of the people unto God. Keep your admonitions for private dealing with the offender, and let your doctrinal instructions go into your sermons. The essence of prayer is asking. The thanksgiving is the acknowledgment of answers already received, and the confession is the preparation for the presenting of new petitions; but the unloading of the heart in earnest, believing supplication, is the great thing that you should seek to accomplish for yourself and for your people in your public approaches to the throne of grace. "Ask and ye shall receive." "Ye have not because ye ask not." Let us only remember these and kindred passages when we rise to lead our people's prayers, and then our aspirations will shape themselves into prayers which will be prayers indeed.

But, passing to another particular, I remark that our public petitions should be real, and not artificial.

We should ask what we and the people truly desire, rather than what we think we ought to desire. There is too much of what might be called mannerism in the prayers of the sanctuary. Certain expressions have come down to us by tradition from the elders, and it has become the fashion to use them, until at length both for him who utters them and the people whom he is leading all meaning has dropped out of them. Nay, sometimes a similar effect has been produced through the formal and habitual adoption even of the language of the Word of God. I trust that I shall not be misunderstood here. The Bible is the great directory in prayer, and there is no liturgy like that of the Book of Psalms. Still, even when we employ its words, we must see to it that we use them intelligently and sincerely, and must not fall into the snare of letting the form become a formalism. We can be whole-souled only in that which is real to us, and to have reality in our petitions, they must be natural and our own. Hence, it is better to use Scriptural quotation only when we can pour our hearts warm and living into its inspired mould; and wherever the language of the Bible is figurative or obscure, we should prefer to put our thought into the plainest words which we can select for ourselves.

The late Dr. James Hamilton has given, in one of his review articles, an interesting illustration, which will make my meaning plain in this connection. He uses it in regard to hymns, but its primary application is to prayer. I quote his words. He says: " I cannot tell it accurately, but I have heard of a godly

couple whose child was sick and at the point of death.
It was unusual to pray together, except at the hour
of 'exercise'; however, in her distress, the mother
prevailed on her husband to kneel down at the bed-
side and 'offer a word of prayer.' The good man's
prayers were chiefly taken from that best of litur-
gies, the Book of Psalms; and after a long and rever-
ential introduction from the 90th psalm and elsewhere, he proceeded: 'Lord, turn again the captivity
of Zion; then shall our mouth be filled with laughter
and our tongue with singing'; and as he was proceeding in that strain, the poor, agonized mother inter-
rupted him, saying: 'Eh! man, you're aye drawn
out for thae Jews, but it's our bairn that's deein',' at
the same time clasping her hands and crying, 'Lord,
help us! oh, give us back our darling, if it be Thy
holy will; and if he is to be taken, oh, take him to
Thyself.' "* Now, every one must see how the reality
of that woman's distress brushed away all mannerism
from her prayer, and she told the Lord just what she
wanted.

But the same thing holds in public petitions. We
have too largely overlaid our devotions, alike in the
sanctuary and the closet, with artificialisms which are
none the less injurious because they consist in the
formal repetition of words taken from the Scriptures
of truth. We attempt to soar aloft into spiritual
regions on the borrowed wings of David and his
brother psalmists, though at the moment we have no

---

* British and Foreign Evangelical Review for 1865, p. 340.

community of feeling with them, and the troubles of our every-day experience are permitted to lie unspoken on our own and our people's hearts. We smile as the lawyer talks of his precedents, and we are apt to say to him: "What of these? Give us justice, and if you have not a precedent, make one for the occasion." We complain of the architect who, forgetting that we are living in the nineteenth century, will insist on building churches for us in the beautiful, yet cold, inconvenient, and dimly-lighted Gothic of the past, and we say to him : " These were all well for former days, but give us something suited to our present requirements." But we are often ourselves guilty of similar anachronisms in our prayers, and keep using forms of expression, some Scriptural and some traditional, which have no special appropriateness to men's circumstances now, until we provoke our people to say, as that agonized mother did, " Use common words that will describe our real needs."

Again, our public prayers should be definite and direct. If we were going on a deputation to the head of some department in the State, and were appointed to represent our companions by making a statement of the case which we had come to plead, we would immediately set ourselves to discover how most pointedly, briefly, and comprehensively we could make our wishes known to the official. All circumlocution would be avoided; we would not ask for anything which we did not want, and we would put clearly and distinctly forward those things which we desired. Now, if we had a right idea of our duty as leaders of public prayer, we would pursue a similar plan with our petitions in the sanctuary. Chalmers said of some one's prayers, that they were "business-like," and he could not have given them higher commendation. When Bartimeus called so loudly and importunately on the Lord to have mercy on him, and Christ commanded that he should be brought unto Him, he was met with the question, "What wilt thou that I should do unto thee?" But he was at no loss for a reply. He did not begin a thousand miles away from the subject that was distressing him, and ask for a great many things for which he did not care, but he went to the point at once, and said: "Lord, that I may receive my sight." So again, when Salome came with her sons, worshiping Him and desiring a certain thing of Him, He said unto her, "What wilt thou?" And in her reply, though she did not know all that was implied in her prayer, she went straight to that which she desired. Now, we may profitably follow such examples; and if, ever as we rise to lead our fellow-worshipers in prayer, we could hear the voice of the Master saying unto us, "What will ye that I should do for you?" our petitions would have as much of definiteness and directness as there is in the flight of an arrow to its mark.

A revival of spiritual life and earnestness in our own souls will richly contribute to the production of this directness. Earnestness always takes the shortest road. "Before our conversion," said some fervent ones, after a revival, "we used to pray in circles, but now we pray in straight lines." I think we might learn much in this respect also from the study of the prayers recorded in the Bible. Take for example that of Abraham's servant when he went for Rebekah, or that of Jacob when he was afraid of meeting Esau, or that of Elijah on Mount Carmel, or that of Peter and the Apostles after the first imprisonment for Jesus' sake, and you will be struck with the simple, honest straightforwardness of the requests they made. These men had an object in view, and they went right onward to that. So let it be with us. Let us gather up the wants of the people as far as they are known to us, and express them simply and truthfully to God, and then let us conclude, and the advantage both in point and brevity will be unspeakable.

Finally, our public prayers should be in some parts intercessory, and not merely selfish. When Christ comes into the heart, He widens it and gives it interest in, and sympathy with, others. Now, these emotions find their natural outlet at the throne of grace. What a beautiful illustration of this we have in the case of the apostle Paul! As in the central office of a great telegraphic company there are wires in communication with all parts of the country and all quarters of the globe, so from the closet of the apostle there went out messages of greeting and benediction, each one going round by the throne of God, to the Christian brethren in all the cities in which he had been permitted to labor. He was a Christian, and was affected by everything that had any slightest influence on the cause of Christ. Therefore, he prayed not only for his brethren in the Lord, but for all men in authority in the state. And in our pulpits we ought to imitate his example. The aged, the sick, the sorrowful, should be remembered by us with tenderness, while those who are laboring in the Sunday-school and mission district should be " commended to the grace of Him in whom they believe." The land we live in should be patriotically borne upon our hearts in public prayer, and our judges, legislators, and magistrates ought never to be forgotten. A place should also frequently be found for the missionary enterprise both at home and abroad, and for the work in which our Tract and Bible societies are so nobly engaged. It will not be wise, indeed, to seek to include all these in every prayer, but by a little system on your part, you may be able so to vary the objects for which you pray on different occasions as to secure brevity and variety at all times. Only remember that the heart must be in each utterance ; for in public prayer, though it is not essential to say all you feel (for *that*, the closet is the place), yet it is indispensable that you feel all you say.

I have not thought it well to say a word on common faults in prayer, partly because these are very faithfully pointed out in various works that are of easy access to you,* and partly because I could not

---

* See, especially, the lectures of the late Dr. Porter, of Andover ; the lecture on Public Prayer in Mr. Spurgeon's " Lectures to my Students ;" and the extremely valuable book on Public Worship, by J. Spencer Pearsall, London.

expose them without seeming to turn very sacred subjects into ridicule. I leave you here, therefore, to the guidance of sanctified common sense and the teachings of the Holy Spirit; and if any one of you should be overwhelmed with a sense of his own unfitness to lead the devotions of others, let him take comfort in the thought that they who have such feelings are most commonly those who excel in this exercise. The poet Cowper shrunk almost from the sound of his own voice, and yet when he led in that little prayer - meeting which was held in the great house of Olney, it is the testimony of those who heard him, that no one ever prayed like him. He who knows that he has a gift in this direction, has in reality no excellence in it, for the consciousness of it mars its glory. He who is eager to lay hold of God, and seeks to rise to ever closer communion with Him, mourning all the while that he is so far from his ideal, is likely to be nearer to it than he wots of. He sees not the shining of his own face, but the people feel that he is 'talking' with God. Take comfort, then, for fluency is not always fervor; and always in prayer there is more real power in the hesitancy of a burdened heart than in the easy utterance of stock phrases. If the heart be in the prayer, other things will right themselves by degrees. But nothing will compensate for the absence of that.

LECTURE XI.

THE PASTORATE AND PASTORAL VISITATION.

LECTURE XI.

THE PASTORATE AND PASTORAL VISITATION.

THE pastorate and the pulpit act and react upon each other. The experiences of the people gathered by the minister in his intercourse among them, serve to enrich his discourses; and the character and conduct of the pastor during the week will either deepen or efface the impressions made by his sermon on the Sabbath. The discourse is itself in some measure a feeding or shepherding of the flock; and the life is always a sermon, for there is no eloquence so potent as that of character, and no influence so subtle as that of example. The sermon of the Lord's day gives the minister an introduction into the homes of his people on other days, and his behavior before them on such occasions will go far either to neutralize or to enforce his public teachings. The deportment of the pastor will be to his discourses, either like the extinguisher, which puts out the light, or like the reflector, which intensifies its lustre.

It is of the utmost importance, therefore, that you should be thoroughly alive to the bearing of your pastoral demeanor on your pulpit efficiency. There are some men of whom you would say, as you listen to their sermons, that they should be always in the pulpit ; but when you meet them in private, you are constrained to declare, as you listen to their conversation, that they should never be in the pulpit. Let it not be so with you. Do nothing in your life to wipe out the impressions made by your sermons, but seek that it may be said of you, as Chaucer said of his " goode parson,"

> " The lore of Christ and his apostles twelve
> He taught, but first he followed it himself."

I would not have you, indeed, to put on any artificial piety, or to cultivate any mere appearance of sanctity. Neither would I desire you to mistake starch for dignity, or moroseness for piety. I have no sympathy with those who seem to think that clergymen are bound by a stricter moral law than other men, and that what is perfectly justifiable in a layman (so-called), is unwarrantable in a minister. We cannot admit that the preacher is to be like a monk, going about with sober step and look demure, never seen to laugh, or if he do make the attempt, that he should only " grin horribly a ghastly smile," and look more melancholy in his mirth than an ordinary mortal would in tears. We grant that he may have some reasons which other men have not, for seeking to walk worthy of the Gospel of Christ ; but every professing Christian should be walking in the same way with him. We grant, also, that he should set an example in every good work ; but that which he sets, if it be really good, it is the duty of his people to follow; and the notion that he ought to be more sedate, subdued, and holy than another Christian should be, is but a fragment of the teaching of that Church which insists upon the celibacy of the clergy, and regards the conventual life as specially "religious." There are not two standards of Christian morality. The pattern is one and the same for all believers; and it is the duty of all alike to get as near as possible to " the measure of the stature of the fullness of Christ."

We ask, therefore, for no professional piety, or official decorum. We desire only that you should cultivate a sense of the presence of Christ with you in all your goings out and comings in among your people, and then everything will come right of itself. Do nothing, and say nothing of which you would be ashamed, if He were visibly by your side; and as when men look at the spectrum through a telescope, they see the mystic presence of other lines than those made by the prismatic colors, so your people, as they scan your deportment, will see in you the evident tokens that there is more about you than merely earthly agencies can account for, even the spirit of the Lord himself.

But mere general exhortation will be comparatively useless to you in this department, and so I will come at once to particulars.

And first, in reference to parish matters, or things pertaining to the management of congregational affairs, let me advise you not to attempt to do too much at the outset of your ministry. Your earliest impulse, as soon as you discover how matters are, will be to set everything right in a moment; and as the young housemaid, in her attempts to clean a room, generally ends by making the confusion greater than it was when she began, the probability is, that you will only increase the difficulties by your efforts to overcome them. Make haste slowly. The first thing you have to do is to attain to ease in the preparation of your discourses. I dare say, you are wondering now how you will ever be able to prepare two sermons weekly. But just similar misgivings have filled the hearts of all your predecessors; and from my experience, I can affirm that a little systematic effort, perseveringly expended, will very soon enable you to accomplish that work within such limits as will allow opportunity for the discharge of other duties. But you will never reach that point if you persist in thinking that you cannot reach it. So you must begin determined to master that difficulty. And, in order to do that thoroughly, you must resist the temptations that will be put before you to induce you to do a great many more things at the same time. These may be very important in their places; but the other is the most important, and they can wait. As John Bright once said, "You can't drive six omnibuses abreast through Temple Bar." Neither can you carry on a great number of different enterprises in the first year or two of your pastorate. Robert Hall was in the habit of saying, that when the devil saw that a young minister was in earnest, he got on his back, and rode him to death, in order

that he might be the sooner rid of him ; and I believe statistics show, that the greatest mortality
among ministers is during the first three years after
settlement. Now one, at least, of the causes of that
is, that most young men put "too many irons into
the fire " at first. Without stopping until their pulpit preparations have become easy to them, they set
up a Bible-class, a cottage-meeting, a mission station,
and so on, and go into each of them with all the
fervor of juvenile enthusiasm, until warned by failing health, when it is too late, they abandon some, or
may have even to look for another sphere. Now you
will not understand that I am an advocate of laziness, when I say that such a course as that is very
bad economy indeed. The sixth commandment is,
" Thou shalt not kill," and it forbids suicide equally
with murder. Therefore, in your pastorate, as in the
ascent of a hill, take it leisurely at first, for if you
run yourself out of breath in the early stages of
your life-journey, you will have no strength re-
maining for the later.

Just before I was settled, I was put on my guard
against this too common besetment of young ministers, by an aged elder who took a fatherly interest in
me. He gave me substantially the advice which I
am repeating now to you. He said, " Keep yourself
entirely for your pulpit work until that becomes
manageable ; then add something else, and when
that has begun to sit lightly upon you, a third enterprise may be taken in hand ; and so you will go on
increasing your influence ; but if you begin all these

things at once, you will inevitably break down, and will have to throw some of them up, thereby giving an aspect of failure to your work which it will never recover." I tried to follow that wise counsel, and to that, by the blessing of God upon me, I trace the fact, that in a ministry of now nearly three and twenty years' duration, I have been incapacitated for public work by illness only for the half of one Sabbath. The health-lift will injure you, if you begin with trying to raise a thousand pounds; but if you commence with a moderate weight, and go on increasing it by the scale, you may, perhaps, come up to the neighborhood of the larger number, and that even with advantage to your physical strength. Now it is quite similar here. Work which, taken gradually upon you, may be performed at length with a sense of invigoration and enjoyment, may kill you, if you undertake it all at once. Let your zeal, therefore, in this department be tempered with discretion.

Again, do not hang everything round your own neck. That was what Moses was doing, when his father-in-law said to him : " Thou wilt surely wear away, both thou and this people that is with thee, for this thing is too heavy for thee, thou art not able to perform it thyself alone," * and counselled him to adopt the principle of the division of labor. Now you ought to follow Jethro's advice. Attempt not to do everything yourself. Train others for work. Study the brethren by whom you are surrounded, and seek

---

* Exodus xviii. 18.

to put each to that for which he is best adapted. It will not do for the commander-in-chief in the day of battle to be mending a broken wagon wheel. He has other and more important work on hand; but such details as that may be left to those who are skilled in setting them to rights. It is your privilege as a minister to plan and superintend the campaign; but you cannot be in every place and do everything. The movements of the battle are to be executed by others. On the Lord's day you give the principles which are to regulate your fellow-laborers, and by the help of God's Spirit, you furnish the enthusiasm by which they are inspired; but you ought not, save in very exceptional cases, as in the beginning of some struggling cause, to be the factotum of the church. Cultivate, therefore, the faculty of organization. Let your church grow under you into a finely-constructed piece of spiritual mechanism, every part of which, as in a steam-engine, shall be nicely adapted to all the rest, and the whole calculated to tell with effect upon the world around, while all you will have to do will be to sustain the water at the boiling point so as to generate the power that is to keep the whole in motion.

Finally, here, do not attempt to have everything done in your own particular way. I have used the illustration of a general with his army, but I did not mean to imply that military discipline could be introduced into the Christian church. Not the commands of the minister, but the precepts of Christ are the orders of the "sacramental host." You must not expect, therefore, that everything will be done precisely as you wish to have it done. You are to move your people by influence, not by authority. If you are a wise man they will not be long in discovering it, and they will defer to you accordingly. But this deference must be mutual, and when you do not see things precisely as they do, then your wisdom will suspect that you may be in the wrong and will lead you gracefully to give way.

Of course, in all this I am referring to modes of operation in which no moral principle is compromised. True disciples of Christ will not insist upon anything that is shown to be contrary to the will of the Lord; but if they should do so, then it will be the right time for you to withstand, and when you resist on such a ground you will be invincible. Such occasions, however, will not be of frequent occurrence; and in all indifferent matters, when your plan is not favored, then be thankful that there are so many people in the church wiser than yourself, and make the best of it. Do not be always acting the part of Cassandra and uttering predictions which nobody believes. Above all, if your prophecies should come to pass, do not turn round and say, "I told you so," but leave the lesson to burn itself in silently, and rely upon it that its influence will be felt for many days. He who is determined at all hazards to have his own will, is lording it over God's heritage, and will get more than he is seeking, for he will bring upon himself the ill-will of the brotherhood, and that will neutralize any amount of pulpit eloquence. It is not a very fitting proverb for an abstainer to quote, yet its appositeness to the case in hand may be excuse enough for repeating the homely saying, " He who will have the last drop in the tankard gets the lid on his nose," and if you are resolved to carry everything according to your will, you will lay up for yourself many a heritage of sorrow. We are the disciples of Him who said, " I am among you as he that serveth," and self in us should be crucified for His sake.

There is another side to all this, no doubt, and if I were lecturing to church members I would insist that they also are bound by these sacred principles; but if there is to be a rivalry as to who should be the first to yield, then let the minister look to his laurels, and see that no man takes his crown.

Passing now to the subject of visitation, I would say that the pastor's first care should be for the aged, the sick, the bereaved, and those who are suffering from any kind of trial. The afflicted long for sympathy, and to whom can they look for that more naturally than to the minister of Christ? Let them not look in vain. Go to them in tenderness and love, with these words sounding in your ears, " Inasmuch as ye have done it unto one of the least of these my brethren, ye have done it unto me." Do not think of such work as if it were a task, or even simply a duty, but esteem it a privilege, and seek " to lift up them that are bowed down."

Let your sympathy be real. Do not say that which you do not feel. But that you may feel rightly, keep yourself in close fellowship with Christ.

While with the one hand you seek to raise your brother out of the depths, put your other into the hand of the Saviour, and seek to imbibe the spirit which He manifested on His visit to the weeping sisters at Bethany.

Consolation will be best imparted by you in the words of Scripture, for at such times there is no solace like that which is contained in the sayings of the Lord Jesus and His inspired servants.   Search the Bible, therefore, for appropriate passages, and that you may have them constantly in readiness, lay them up in the memory of the heart.   They will be always more powerful when you have found them for yourself; but that you may know what a treasury of comfort there is laid up in these ancient oracles, and how it may be turned to account in dealing with modern sufferers, such a book as that of Andrew Bonar,* the biographer of McCheyne, may be very valuable and suggestive.

Sometimes, indeed, it may seem to you that even the words of inspiration will fall like hail-stones on the sufferer's heart, and you may be fain to take refuge in silence, solacing yourself the while with Whittier's lines:

> " With silence only as their benediction
>   God's angel's come ;
>   When in the shadow of a great affliction
>   The soul sits dumb."

* The Visitor's Book of Texts ; or, The Word brought nigh to the sick and sorrowful. By the Rev. A. A. Bonar. London : Nisbet & Co.

But even in that unbroken stillness there will be comfort, if the tear shall be seen standing in the eye, and if, at length, the quiet voice of prayer tenderly pleading with God, shall rise out of the darkness. On such occasions be not in too much haste to check the outburst of grief, or to point the practical lesson of the trial. Wait a little, and ere long a blessed opportunity will come which you may turn to the best account both for the mourner and for your Lord.

Then when you enter the chamber of the sick one, cultivate the gentleness of your Master. " Do not strive, nor cry, nor lift up your voice." Go with muffled footstep into the room. Speak softly and tenderly. Lead the sufferer to Christ. Pray with him, and in all your exercises let a holy cheerfulness surround you like a halo. Be not sombre or gloomy. Let the sick one and his nurse feel as if a ray of sunlight had come in to gladden them. Do not remain so long as to create fatigue, and thus your visits will do "good like a medicine," and your return will be looked for with eagerness.

If the illness is mortal, realize the responsibility of the position in which you stand, yet do not rashly and bluntly perform that which is much better accomplished by the method of indirectness. Relatives will perhaps insist that you should inform the sufferer that his recovery is hopeless; and though I have always felt, that in so doing they lay upon us a burden which we ought not to be called to bear, yet in such circumstances you ought lovingly and gently to lead the mind of the afflicted one to the contemplation of his departure;

and if he be unconverted, to the consideration of the
urgency of his repentance and return to God. It is a
solemn work; yet trusting in the help of the Holy
Spirit, you may be enabled to perform it in such a
way as to bring home the wanderer even at the
eleventh hour. Be faithful, be tender, be true both
to the sinner and his Saviour, and you will in no wise
lose your reward.

Nor are the benefits of such ministrations to the
sorrowful and the sick restricted to those to whom
especially they are rendered. They will open to you
the hearts of all the members of the household. A
new love for you and for your work will be born within their souls, and by a little wisdom on your part,
you may be blessed in leading them all into the fold.
Your public discourses at such times will be much
more interesting to them than they ever were before;
your words will fall into the furrows which God's
afflictions have made in their hearts and the profiting
will appear after many days. Your kindness at such a
season will never be forgotten, and always your most
devoted friends, and those who profit most by your
labors in the pulpit, will be those whom you have
visited and comforted in their affliction. The longer
a minister is with his people, he sees the more of
them in such tribulation; and thus it is, if he be
faithful to his trust, that their hearts twine around
him, and he seems at length to belong to every
family among them. How strong such ties are, only
he can tell, who after they have increasingly encircled
him for many years, is compelled to break them at

the call of the Master, and to begin his work anew among those whom he has never seen. The pain of that heart-wrench is in me yet scarcely healed; but the love which caused the pain is indestructible, because it is the evidence that the services tenderly rendered on the one side, were gratefully received on the other, and that the issue was the profit of both My young brethren, be much in the homes of sorrow, for through your ministrations to the afflicted, your pulpit utterances will acquire increasing power.

On the subject of general systematic visitation of your people, perhaps a history of my own experience may be more helpful to you than any series of formal exhortations. I was first settled over a church of about one hundred and eighty members, many of whom resided in the village in which the place of worship was situated, but a considerable number of whom were farmers, scattered over an area of about six miles in length, by about two in breadth. I made my visits systematically week by week, taking the parish in manageable districts. At first I was accompanied on each occasion by an elder. It was expected that I should ask a few questions of the children, assemble the members of the household, give a formal address, and then conclude with prayer. The presence of the "lay brother" was a great embarrassment. I supposed that because he was with me I should have a new address in every house, and should have a prayer in every instance perfectly distinct from any which I had formerly offered. I had not then heard of the shrewd device by which a minister in one of the largest cities in Scotland had got rid of his encumbering companion. He endured the affliction patiently for one day, but on the following week, when it came to the time that prayer should be offered in the first house visited, he turned to his friend and said, " Mr. ——, will you pray?" and when he had repeated that request in two or three households, Mr. —— discovered that he had an engagement in the city, and disappeared. In those early days, however, I was too unsophisticated to think of doing anything like that, so I went on from house to house, making a new address in each, until, when it was towards evening, and I had walked perhaps five or six miles, and made ten or twelve addresses, I was more dead than alive. You cannot wonder, that in these circumstances, pastoral visitation became the " *bête noir* " of my life, and I positively hated it. Thus prosecuted, it was simply and only drudgery, and so far as I know, was not productive of any good result.

When I removed to Liverpool I began in a different way. I made no public announcement of my purpose to visit in any street or locality, but kept steadily before me a certain systematic plan, by which I was enabled to get round all the families under my care in a reasonable time. I gave up all formal addressing, and went into each home as a friend and brother in the Lord ; and then when I had regained my liberty, my joy returned. I made it my business to find out the experiences through which the household had passed since I had been last in it. As opportunity offered, not obtrusively and professionally, but naturally and incidentally, I dropped a word for the Master, and at the close of the visit I attempted to gather up into a brief prayer those supplications which I judged to be most appropriate to the circumstances which our conversation had revealed.

Thus I went on for several years, when I discovered that although I was earnestly doing everything I could, I was yet, somehow, failing to satisfy either my own conscience or my people's expectations in the matter of visiting. I was continually asking myself whether I could not do more; and each person who did not see me in his house during the week, imagined that as I had not been to visit him, I had not been to see anybody else. So, on looking all round the situation, I determined, while preserving the informal character of the visitation, to make public announcement on the Sabbath, of the day and the district which I meant to take.

The advantages of this plan were numerous. It kept me up to the mark, for having once made the engagement, no light thing was permitted to interfere with its being carried out. Formerly, if a friend happened to call on me on the day and at the hour on which in my own mind I had fixed for visitation, I was tempted to say, "Well, the visiting can stand over;" and I remained with him, leaving arrears of work to accumulate often to a very serious extent. But now the programme was carried out, no matter who should come in at the moment, or what might be the state of the weather. Again, it enabled me to keep the specified day free from all other pastoral engagements. If a wedding came to be arranged for, the hour was fixed, so as not to interfere with the purpose already publicly made known; if a funeral was to be conducted, the time was appointed so as to leave this other work untouched. Thus the intimation of my intention to spend a certain day in visiting in a certain locality, cleared the way for its being carried out. It was an express train, for which all the minor accommodation trains had to give place; and so it happened that at the year's end it reached its destination, having lost no time on the road, and all the passengers were satisfied.

Moreover, the public announcement had this incidental advantage, of which at first I had not thought, namely, that it stopped at once all grumbling on the part of the unvisited. They saw that I was steadily working week by week somewhere; it became a matter of interest to them to watch my progress, and they looked with a certain strange eagerness for the day when I should name the street in which they resided. I do not know that in the long run I actually did much more pastoral work than I was doing before, but I accomplished it with more ease to myself, and with far more satisfaction to my people.

When I came to New York I resumed this practice in every particular, save that I found it was not always convenient to offer prayer; and thus far it has wrought admirably, for if it were not for the interruption of the summer Hegira, and for such absorbing engagements as that of delivering "Lectures on Preaching" here and there over the country, I would get over my parish in little more than eight or nine months.

But that is only an external history. You want to know how to deal with the people themselves in visiting them. First, then, shun all stiffness and formality. Never mind your dignity; think of your Master, and go everywhere out of love to Him. "Turn your hand upon the little ones." Be not so pompous and formidable that the children will run to hide themselves at your approach. There was a whole volume of pastoral theology in the reply of the Highland shepherd to the question how it came that he took so many prizes for the best flock at the cattle shows. He said, "I look weel to the lambs." So look you well to the lambs. Encourage them to come to you; and by your tenderness to them, you will easily enter into their parents' hearts.

Be natural and affable. Do not surround yourself with *chevaux de frise* as if you were a marble statue in the midst of a crowded thoroughfare; but let your heart be open and your words be free. And while you will never allow yourself to forget that you are there in the name of the Lord, do not drag in the subject of religion in such a way as to make the whole matter distasteful. Cultivate the art of incidental allusion, and if you make a transition in the conversation, make it naturally, so that everybody will not be jolted into silence. We must find out that in which our friends are interested, and descending to their level therein, we shall be able to lift them more easily to that which we desire to set before them.   A friend told me that he went one evening into the room where his son was taking lessons in singing, and found the tutor urging him to sound a certain note.   Each time the lad made the attempt, however, he fell short, and the teacher kept on saying to him, "Higher! higher!"   But it was all to no purpose, until, descending to the tone which the boy was sounding, the musician accompanied him with his own voice, and led him gradually up to that which he wanted him to sing, and then he sounded it with ease.

You have heard the story of Edward Irving and the infidel shoe-maker who seemed resolutely bent on refusing to hold any communication with him.   Going up to his "seat," Irving lifted a piece of patent-leather, which was then a recent invention, and, as his father was a tanner, he knew so much about it that he was able to speak intelligently regarding it; the "sutor" continued at his work, preserving silence as long as he could, until exasperated by what he thought the pretension of the minister, he asked: "What do ye ken aboot leather?"   Irving, in reply, went into the whole subject, and, after a time, won by his acquaintance with the matter of his craft, the shoe-maker said: "You're a decent kind o' fellow; do *you* preach?" On the following Sabbath the vanquished cobbler made his appearance for the first time at church, and became a regular attendant on Irving's ministry, excusing himself to all who wondered at his conduct by saying, "He's a sensible man yon, he kens aboot leather!"*

Now, an incident like that indicates that in order to turn pastoral visitation to good account we must interest ourselves in the common labors and experiences of our people, and enter through that door into their hearts. I was one evening driven home from a farmer's house, a distance of some six or seven miles, by a frank young boy, who at once got into conversation with me. He talked about the farm, the horses and the dog, and then by some subtle link of association the subject was changed to that of the school. I soon discovered that his favorite study was arithmetic, and asked him what he was doing in it: "O," he replied, "I am in profit and loss." "Can you do all the examples in it?" "Yes, some of them were very hard, but I have done them all; I did the last to-day." "I think I could give you one in that rule that you could not do." "I doubt it; let me hear it." "It is this: 'What shall it profit a man if he should gain the whole world and lose his own soul?' Could you work that out?" "No," said he, as a thoughtful expression came over his countenance; "that's beyond me, I admit." Thus, having won his confidence and affection, it was easy for me to speak with him in such a way that his whole nature was aroused, and by and by he gave himself to the Lord.

_____

* See "The Life of Edward Irving," by Mrs. Oliphant, pp. 110, 111.

Or, to take another illustration: Suppose I enter a house, in which are many beautiful engravings; among these there is one of Holman Hunt's deeply suggestive painting, "The Light of the World," and from that it is easy to pass to the text which the picture illustrates: "Behold I stand at the door and knock." Or I may tell the following story about the artist who produced the work: Some seven or eight summers ago a distinguished non-conformist divine of England was a guest in the house of the gentleman who now owns the original painting. At the time of his visit the picture was undergoing the process of re-framing, and so he was permitted to examine it minutely. In one of the lower corners, where the words would in ordinary circumstances have been covered by the frame, he found in the handwriting of the artist himself this expression : " *Nec me praetermittas Domine,*" " Nor pass·me by, O Lord ! " and so from the prayer of the painter a very natural lesson, all the more powerful because of its incidental character, may be read to the possessor of the engraving.

To succeed in such work as this, however, we must cultivate general intelligence, and be ever on the watch for incidents and illustrations which we may use thus as we go from house to house. "Parlor preaching" is in its own place only inferior in importance to "pulpit preaching." It needs great wealth of resources, and, most of all, it requires that habitual spiritually-mindedness which is holding fellowship with Christ even in the commonest occupations. You will never succeed in your visitation if you go to it with an effort, and as a duty. But when you start out for the love of Jesus, and in His name, your exercise will be a joy to yourself and full of profit to thóse on whom you call.

Nor will the benefit of it be only direct. It will bring the families whom you have seen, with new interest to the sanctuary, and put their minds into a state of greater impressibility. They are no longer at arm's length from you. They have grasped your hand, they have heard your heart-throb in their homes, and now your words take stronger hold upon their souls. John Brown's ' Jeames' said, in regard to prayer, " There is no good done till we come to close grips with God." But it is just as true in regard to preaching that we do little for men until we get into personal dealing with them. If I am firing at a target with a rifle, I want to know whether I have hit the bull's-eye. And if I am in earnest in preaching on the Lord's day, I desire to discover whether any results have followed. Now it is only through pastoral visitation that I can follow up my sermons. Thus, while in some cases it lets me see where I can drive a nail to advantage, in others it enables me to clinch a nail which I have already driven.

You will make a great mistake, therefore, if you undervalue the visitation of your people. The pulpit is your throne, no doubt ; but then a throne is stable only when it rests on the affections of the people, and to get their affections you must visit them in their dwellings. I used to look upon my visitation as a dreadful drudgery, but it has now become my joy ;

so that whenever I am tempted to despond I sally forth to visit my flock; and as I look sadly back upon those early years in which I had no such gladness, I am earnestly desirous to save you from blundering as I did.

Begin this work as your pastorate begins. If you cannot fully master your pulpit preparations at first, so as to secure the time needful for systematic visitation, yet never omit the care of the sick and the afflicted; and at the earliest possible moment enter upon the regular prosecution of this important department of your labors. It will "mellow and fatten" the roots of your own character. It will feed your public prayers. It will furnish many themes and suggestions for your pulpit teachings. It will cheer you on in a thousand ways in your arduous exertions, and as the years revolve you will come to be regarded almost as a member of every family, and be rewarded by the confidence and affection of the flock as a whole. On that you may always rest as securely as the swimmer does upon the wave; and your character among your people will add an irresistible ingredient to the eloquence of your speech.

LECTURE XII.

THE RELATION OF THE PULPIT TO PRESENT QUESTIONS.

LECTURE XII.

THE RELATION OF THE PULPIT TO PRESENT QUESTIONS.

HE who would be successful in the ministry of the Word must give himself wholly to it. When the apostles responded to the Master's call "they forsook all and followed Him;" and no one who is really called to the work of the pastorate will be able to combine with that any other occupation. When Chalmers was first settled at Kilmany he tried to unite with his ministry the teaching of mathematics and chemistry at St. Andrews, and assured his father that Saturday was sufficient for the preparation of his discourses. But after he had passed the great crisis of his life, he was constrained to devote every moment of his time and every energy of his being to the duties of his office. And every earnest pastor will feel as he then did. No one who has any right idea of the importance of the ministry, will consent to regard it as a merely secondary or subordinate thing. He will not be able to satisfy himself with less than unreserved consecration to his calling; and if he is to preach sermons that will compel men to listen to them, they must be the product of his un-distracted labor. The river of the week must flow with undivided current into the pulpit. He must live, and move, and have his being, in and for his work.

He cannot afford, as a regular thing, to become a peripatetic lecturer, or to be the principal of an educational establishment, or to conduct a newspaper, or to devote himself to some field of scientific inquiry. He may have sufficient ability to do both things. He may even, by dint of good management and hard work, contrive to secure time enough for both. But his heart will be divided between them, and that will be fatal to his efficiency in the pulpit. His ministry *must* have the whole of him, else ere long the "unction" will evaporate out of his speech, and the spell of his eloquence will be broken.

He who desires success as a preacher, therefore, must be content to leave many other things alone. He may have dreamed in early years of winning fame in the republic of letters, or of rising to eminence in some scientific pursuit, but all such ambitions must now be given up for Christ. The prizes of commerce and the honors of statesmanship are not for him. He has been called to labor in another field, whereon the harvests are immortal souls; and so eager is he in its cultivation, that he cannot consent to give any part of himself to other engagements. So soon as he does that, the joy of his heart will disappear, and the glory of his ministry will depart.

Be it yours, therefore, uncompromisingly to resist every overture that may be made to you to give any part of your time and strength, as a constant thing, to any other object than your ministry. The sucker in the end will kill the tree; therefore take heed that it be not permitted to spring up. It were better that you should renounce the ministry altogether than that you should continue in it half-heartedly, giving the greater part of your time and thoughts to something else than the feeding and shepherding of the flock of God.

But though I would urge you to keep yourself exclusively to your calling, I would not have you to adopt a narrow or restricted idea of that calling. You have range enough in the pulpit to satisfy any ordinary ambition; and it is at once your privilege and your duty there to bring the principles and motives of the Gospel of Christ to bear upon the circumstances of your times, and the questions that are agitating the minds of men.

Thus there are many social subjects intimately connected with the welfare of the people, which not only may be treated of, but which ought to be treated of, in the pulpit. Foremost among these is the condition of a large proportion of the poorer classes of the land, who, in popular speech, are called the masses. What ignorance, intemperance, immorality, and crime prevail among them! We talk of heathenism with horror, but there are multitudes almost at our own doors, and within the sound of our church bells, who are living in circumstances as debasing as any to be found in pagan lands. The car of Juggernaut has not crushed as many victims as intemperance is annually destroying in our cities; and India has no cruelties more horrid than those which are almost nightly committed by the criminal classes in our country. What dens of infamy and homes of sin there are in all our cities, infecting by their impurity even the households of those who are themselves ashamed even to name the abominations of which they are the scene!

Then in another department, who among us has not been filled with sad forebodings for the future, as he has marked the growing conflict between capital and labor, and the ever increasing estrangement between employers and employed, now rumbling ominously like some far-off earthquake, and now breaking out into the volcanic eruption of a disastrous strike? While at the other extremity of the social scale, the luxury and extravagance, the ostentatious rivalry in the keeping up of appearances, the heartless worldliness, and the grasping selfishness, are utterly appalling.

Now these are things that the Christian preacher cannot pass by on the other side. He has been made a minister for the very purpose of grappling with them, and it will be treachery to his office and treason to his Lord, if he refuse to deal with them. They threaten the very life of the nation, and he is set upon the watch-tower for the very purpose of giving an alarm. Some one has compared the republic under which we live to a pyramid, having its base composed of the great masses of the people, and rising up, narrowing as it rises, through legislatures, judges, and governors, until it finds its apex in him who sits in the presidential chair; and it is alleged that this is the most stable form of government. And so it is, if the pyramid be composed of the most enduring materials. But if the base be honey-combed with intemperance, the central portions corroded with extravagance, and the upper layers disintegrated by dishonesty, how long will the whole fabric last?

But more even than the welfare of the nation is endangered by the social evils of which we speak. They imperil also the life of the church. Its members cannot live in the neighborhood of such things without being in some degree contaminated. If malaria is in the district, you cannot confine it to one house. Its influence enters more or less into every dwelling. And the Church and the State are not so completely separated, even in this land, that the one cannot be affected by the other. Their very proximity to each other makes the danger of the one a peril also to the other. I went once with a friend into his garden, and, observing in one part of it, a plentiful crop of a very troublesome weed, I asked him how he came to have so much of it. He said, "My neighbor was absent from his house three months last year, and let his garden run wild; it was just at the time when that particular weed was running to seed, and the wind blew the downy things over here. It would have paid me to have hired a man to clean his garden for him, but then, you see, I did not think of it in time." So, be sure, if we in the church allow those evils in the community to go on unchecked, the seeds that spring from them will blow over into our own garden, and produce there confusion and every evil work.

How long will our cities be safe places for the godly upbringing of our sons and daughters, if we permit the impurity and iniquity in which they abound to grow rampant in the midst of them? The life of the church, therefore, depends on its aggressiveness, and the ministers of the Gospel must lead forth their people to this new crusade. We must not allow our hearers to rest contented in the thought that if only they are benefited, and gratified, and comforted by our discourses, and labors in the midst of them, there is nothing else to be desired. We must rouse them to a sense of their duty to those around them who are perishing for lack of knowledge; we must urge them on, by the highest and holiest considerations, to prayer and liberality, and personal exertion for the welfare of the fallen and degraded in the land; and as occasion offers, we must give ourselves enthusiastically to evangelistic work in the streets or lanes by which our stately churches are surrounded.

For the Gospel which we preach is the only remedy that can meet the manifold evils of society. All these are only so many different symptoms of the one disease of sin, and nothing can permanently remove *them* save that which eradicates *it*. Hence the various agencies which men have proposed and experimented with for the purpose of improving the condition of the masses, valuable as they have been in some respects, have failed to get at the source of the evil. They have "skinned and filmed the ulcerous sore," but left the constitutional malady, of which it was the symptom, to break out in some other direction. They have dammed up the stream for a little, and sent its waters over into places which were before uncovered; but they have not dried up the fountain-head. The only thing which can regenerate society, is that which can regenerate the individual heart, to wit, the power of the Holy Ghost working in and through the belief of the truth as it is in Jesus. Now as we are set not merely for the defence, but also for the diffusion of that truth, it is imperative on us that we stir up both ourselves and our people, to take means for proclaiming it to the outcasts around us. We must "go out into the streets and lanes of the cities, and compel them to come in." Most evidently we ministers cannot personally carry on such a work, and at the same time satisfy all the demands that are made upon us as pastors, especially if our pastorate should happen to be in a great city. But it is not necessary that we should. Our object ought to be to stimulate every Christian to become himself a home missionary; and to furnish him, week by week, with truth appropriate for his use in that capacity, and with motive strong enough to sustain him in its proclamation. We should aim so to preach that no idler can remain comfortable under our ministrations, and we should seek by a wise organization to realize the ideal of Wesley in our church, "At work, all at work, and always at work." EVERY BELIEVER A MISSIONARY; that must be our watchword, and then our Sabbath services will be the rallying points at which we come together to recruit our wearied energies, and from which we go forth with new enthusiasm to our holy work. Admirably has it been said by the author of "Ecce Homo": "Men who meet within the church walls on Sunday, should not meet as strangers who find themselves together in the same lecture hall; but as co-operators in a public work, the object of which all understand, and to his own department of which each man habitually applies mind and his contriving power. Thus meeting, with the *esprit de corps* strong among them, and with a clear perception of the purpose of their union and their meeting, they would not desire that the exhortation of the preacher should be what in the nature of things it seldom can be—eloquent. . . . It might then become weighty with business, and impressive as an officer's address to his troops before a battle. For it would be addressed by a soldier to soldiers, in the presence of an enemy whose character they understood, and in a war with whom they had given and received telling blows." *

But even when we have got all our people up to the working point, there will be need for some central agency round which their operations must be conducted; and I cannot but think that the enterprise which Christian men are now carrying on in the city of New York, is designed, in the Providence of God, to lead to some developments in home missionary matters which shall be fraught with blessing to the land.

---

* "Ecce Homo," pp. 225, 226.

For one thing it has shown, that the lowest stratum of the population can be reached with the Gospel. In conversation with a friend the other day, I learned that the missionary who labors in the Tombs, informed him that the number of prisoners was smaller than it had been for a long time, and he traced that state of things to the fact that the roughs of the city were attending at the Hippodrome, and so were at least kept out of mischief thereby. And this testimony was strikingly confirmed by one of the police who are in regular waiting at the Hippodrome. He told my informant that on the first night of the services, he was positively alarmed to see such a collection of the " hardest " criminals of the city in the section of the hall under his care. He feared that they might attempt some outbreak, but they sat quietly all through, and the greater number of them come now every night. Another friend mentioned to me that while he was in the inquiry-room a man came to him in great distress, under the deepest conviction of sin, saying to him, " I did not come here to seek salvation; I came to pick pockets; but the Lord has laid hold of me, and I mean to turn to Him." Now these incidents show that the people *can* be reached. They will come to hear the Gospel when they have a fitting opportunity, and the Gospel is in their case also " the power of God unto salvation."

Again, these services show that some men are better qualified than others for reaching these classes. It is needless to attempt to analyze the elements of Mr. Moody's and Mr. Sankey's power. They are

men, I believe, as truly raised up by God for their
work as were Wesley and Whitefield, Nettleton and
Finney; and their success is their attestation.   Now
does not this indicate to us that when a man shows
such eminent fitness for this particular work, he should
be at once laid hold of, and statedly employed in it?
We have got into certain ecclesiastical ruts, and are
in danger of sacrificing life to order.   Why should we
not, however, have even this great benefit in an
orderly way?   There are men who could do nothing
or next to nothing as pastors, who would yet be beyond all price as peripatetic evangelists.   What
hinders that they should be at once recognized in
that character, and sent forth from city to city and
from village to village, two and two, like the first disciples?   It seems to me that if such a plan were
adopted, we might have, not in one city only, but in
every city of the Union, some earnest and attractive
man of God laboring with a power only second to
that which is attending the Lord's messengers in
New York to-day.

Still farther, these services show that Christian co-
operation between the members of different denominations is a possible thing.   In the inquiry-rooms at
the Hippodrome you will find Episcopalians, Baptists,
Methodists, Presbyterians, Congregationalists, all
earnestly at work in seeking to point souls to Christ.
Now if all this may last for two months, why should
it not last for years?   Could we not have a permanent Hippodrome in New York, supplied by men
whom God may raise up, and officered, as it is to-

day, by Christians of all evangelical denominations? And have we not in this a gleam of light thrown upon that darkest, saddest social problem of our times, how to elevate the masses of our large cities?

But whatever else may or may not be done, thus much is clear, that every minister should stir up his people to personal exertion in this great cause. You may say, indeed, that he cannot be always preaching upon it; and if you mean by that, that he is not to be expected to be continually discoursing set sermons on the evil of intemperance and how to meet it, or on the claims of the non-church-going population on the attention of the church, or on the different branches of that upas tree which is poisoning our social life, you are probably right. That course might aggravate and irritate, instead of stimulating to work. But while he may occasionally preach an entire sermon upon some one particular evil, and show how the Gospel is to be brought to bear upon it, he will be wiser if he deal with all such questions incidentally, and if after he has conclusively established some general principles, he should turn unexpectedly upon his hearers and show them how these are to be applied to present circumstances. It is just here, indeed, that he will be able to turn his habit of consecutive exposition to most valuable account. For no matter where he begins such a work, he will not go on very far without finding some excellent opportunity of saying something on these social subjects that may "strike and stick." He can scarcely open the very first book of Scripture without coming upon the excuse of the

selfish fratricide, "Am I my brother's keeper?" and
he will be no faithful shepherd if he do not from that
expose the Cain-like spirit of too many of our modern
hearers of the Gospel.   Not many chapters more shall
have passed before he confronts the drunkenness of
Noah and Lot, and the fearful consequences that
sprung out of the defilement of Dinah, and in these he
will have unsought and incidental opportunities for
the proclamation of truths, which are too often utterly
ignored in the pulpit.   So again, if he take up the
sweet pastoral of Ruth, he will not go far until he
hear the mutual greeting of Boaz and his reapers
when he said unto them, "The Lord be with you,"
and they answered him, "The Lord bless thee," and
that will give him scope enough for treating the whole
question as between employers and employed, and
suggest the true and only remedy, namely, the common brotherhood of both in the Lord.   And if he go
on through the history of the Kings, he may find a
lesson for the ostentation of the times in the fact that
the display which Hezekiah made of his treasures before the eyes of the Assyrian ambassadors was immediately followed by the invasion of the Assyrian
host.

If he should open the New Testament, he cannot
expound the Sermon on the Mount without coming
down with withering power upon the evils of the
times; or enforce the parable of the Good Samaritan
without stirring up his people to sacrifice their money
and their comfort for the good of others.   In a word,
he cannot stand beneath the cross and contemplate

the sacrifice which Christ made there for sinners of mankind, without crying out himself, and leading others to cry out, " What shall I render to the Lord for all His benefits?" and they cannot present such a prayer sincerely without having their eyes opened to see the poor half-dead ones whom sin has wounded and cruelty has scarred, lying all around, waiting for a brother's help. Thus his pulpit will become a center of influence, the results of which may tell on thousands whom he has never seen. My young brethren, aim at making your pulpits such centers; take as your motto the words of Robert Nicol when he left his Perthshire home for the editorial chair, " We'll make the world better yet." Shake off all slothfulness and indifference. Go forth, trusting in the might, and the majesty, and the grace of Him whom you serve, and He will make you the means of salvation to multitudes. Linger not, for while you delay, souls are going down to an undone eternity. Falter not, for greater is He that is in you than he that is in the world ; and when men would urge you to sit still, make answer in the words of the noble Port Royalist, " What! shall we not have a whole eternity to rest in?" or in the loftier words of the Master himself, " I must work the work of him that sent me while it is day; the night cometh when no man can work."

But there is another class of subjects concerning which it may be well to define somewhat precisely the province of the pulpit. I refer now to the political.

The Christian is a citizen as well as a saint, and he should manifest his piety in the discharge of his civic duties. Hence it is clearly within the range of the pulpit to insist occasionally on the importance of Christians taking a practical interest in political matters. It has come to pass among us that all such things are left, I will not say exclusively, but largely, to those who have no regard for the Gospel of Christ ; and so the whole class of men who engage in them is brought under reproach. Now that is a sore evil, not only for the State, but for the Church. The State cannot be entrusted to the management of such men without suffering detriment ; and the members of the Church cannot live in the habitual neglect of a positive duty without entailing some injury upon themselves. Let the minister, therefore, when a fitting opportunity comes, exhort Christians earnestly to assume their proper responsibility as citizens. Let him show that it is as much a privilege and a duty to take part in the details of civil government, as it is to participate in the ordinances of religious worship ; and let him exhort all to take their Christianity with them in the exercise of their civil rights, and to go to the ballot-box with as thorough a resolution to serve God there as they make when they are going to the communion table. This is the only way to purify our political life ; and if the ministers of the Gospel shall not urge their people to adopt it, how is relief to be obtained ? " Ye are the salt of the earth : but if the salt have lost its savor, wherewith shall *it* be salted ? it is thenceforth good for nothing but to be cast out and trodden under foot of men."

But, while it is the duty of the preacher thus to seek to purify and elevate political life, by showing that it is only one department of Christian activity, he must not use his pulpit in the interests of any party in the State. He is a citizen as well as other men, and ought to avail himself of his privileges as such, but it is a fair matter for argument whether or not he should ever allow himself to become prominent on either of the two sides into which politicians are divided. It is conceivable, however, that the questions under discussion may have such moral and religious bearings that he feels compelled to use his influence for one rather than another, and at such a time he may, in my judgment, give public utterance to his sentiments, and seek to enforce the reasons which have commended them to his adoption. But he must not do so in the pulpit. He must go for such a purpose to the political platform, and take his chance of being met by counter-argument or demonstrations of dissent. The pulpit gives no opportunity of reply to the hearer; and it is not only unseemly, but unfair for its occupant to take advantage of the battlements within which he is there entrenched for the firing of a party gun. Let him have the courage of his convictions, and go with his speech where men can hiss at him or answer him if they choose. But let him not request people to come to the sanctuary for the worship of God, and then take advantage of the fact that he has it all his own way, for " pitching in " to them on some political question. His appearance in the political arena will be all the more effective if it be known that he has kept all partizanship out of the house of God.

There may be exceptional times, as when the crisis of some great agony or conflict is upon the nation, when it may be imperative on the preacher to take the matter with him into the pulpit; but in all ordinary cases when he carries party politics into the sanctuary he is doing a certain evil for the attainment of an uncertain good, which, after all, even if certain, might be as well attained elsewhere. He may please some, but he will undoubtedly so irritate others as to turn them away from him even when he is dealing in those faithful sayings which are " worthy of all acceptation."

Some will say that by giving this advice I am advocating a cowardly policy. But it is quite otherwise. The cowardice will consist in the minister's sheltering himself behind the safeguards of the pulpit. It is an easy thing to be vehement and demonstrative, and even defiant, when a man knows that nobody then present has the right to peep or mutter either in dissent or in reply. The true courage will consist in going to fight the battle, where a battle is possible— on the political platform, and seeking there to win the day for truth, for purity, and for freedom.

Even that, however, should be the rare exception with the minister of Christ, and he should take such a course only when some sacred right of humanity is assailed, or some moral principle is in danger of being violated, or some matter of religious liberty and equality is imperilled.

Generally speaking, he will serve the nation best by

adhering to his high spiritual vocation ; for the prosperity of the country depends on the character of
the people, and nothing can make and mould character like the Gospel of Christ.

But I pass now to an entirely different class of
questions, which in their own department are not less
important than those to which I have already alluded.
I mean those which have been developed by the advancement of science. It has been alleged that the
statements of the Word of God are inconsistent with
the discoveries of our physical philosophers.

Now, here, my first counsel is, that in relation to
all such subjects the preacher should not be an
alarmist. Do not give your people the idea that the
revelation of God is endangered by every fragment
of a "jaw-bone" that may be discovered at "Abbe-
ville" or elsewhere. Be open and receptive towards
sicence. If on its own evidence the Bible is true, you
may be sure that in the end no other truth can harm
it. It betrays weakness in the defenders of the Word
of God when they are so excited about little things.
Besides, they have no need to be afraid. The fact of
Christ's resurrection from the dead is not to be imperilled by any question concerning chronology or the
antiquity of the race.

Again, do not be always attacking scientific men.
Nothing has been more painful to me in listening to
discourses, especially from young men, than to hear
the light and flippant tone in which some of the
greatest discoverers of the age were alluded to.

They communicated the impression that there is some special affinity between science and infidelity. But that is very far, indeed, from being the case. The noble Faraday was as conspicuous for his humble faith in the Lord Jesus Christ as he was for his marvellous researches into magnetism and its related sciences; and during the meetings of the British Association for the Advancement of Science, a year or two ago, at Edinburgh, there were maintained by some of its members, morning gatherings for prayer, as remarkable in their character as those which are held at the anniversary of the American Board among ourselves. Therefore, it is not only ungenerous, but untrue, to insinuate that science inevitably leads to scepticism.

Furthermore, do not attempt to answer any of the objections raised by some men of science, unless you have fully and fairly mastered the subject from their point of view. It is unfortunate that on each side of this modern debate, much ignorance prevails regarding the department of the other. Scientific investigators have not had a theological training. The tendency of their pursuits, as Jouffroy has well said, is "to concentrate all their minds in their eyes and hands." They are apt, therefore, to have no proper appreciation of moral evidence, and to ignore the intuitions of the soul itself. But in theologians we have just the opposite evil. They have had no scientific training, and in their vivid realization of the importance of spiritual truth, they are apt to depreciate the labors of the physical philosopher. Now, in these circumstances it will be foolish, not to say fool-hardy, in you to attack the positions of the man of science, unless you are equally familiar with the subject with himself. The true mediators here must be men who can lay their hands upon both parties, and who have the piety of the Christian, combined with the insight and comprehension of the man of science. It will be well, therefore, to leave the harmonizing of the two to such men as are equally at home in both departments. A lumbering and ineffective reply is a thousand times worse than none; and if you cannot speak with the authority of conclusiveness, the best thing you can do is to lead sinful souls to Christ, and let them receive from Him such experimental evidence of the reality of His salvation as no power of infidelity will ever shake.

But, without attempting to answer the objections which have been raised from modern discovery, you may do good service occasionally by pointing out where precisely the discrepancies emerge. The scientific man believes in the infallibility of nature; the theologian believes in the infallibility of Scripture; and the differences, of which so much is made in these days, lie, not between nature and revelation in themselves, but between human interpretations of them. The man of science interprets his facts in a certain way, and makes certain deductions from them. These interpretations and deductions, however, are not infallible; they are not yet all unquestioningly received by scientific men themselves. It is too soon, therefore, to speak and reason, as if they were absolutely correct.

Again, the theologian's interpretations of Scripture are by no means infallible. Many of them which were accepted in past days, have been disproved and others substituted for them; and of many more it must be said that they are still unsettled. For instance, he would be a rash man who should assert that he has discovered, with infallible accuracy, the meaning of the first chapter of Genesis; or should affirm that he can satisfactorily unravel the chronology of the early chapters of that book. These questions, and many others like them, are still *sub judice*, and the wise course for all parties to this modern misunderstanding is to wait, with mutual respect for each other, until God, in His providence and by His spirit, shall lead to such interpretations of nature on the one hand and of Scripture on the other, as shall make manifest their perfect harmony. Let the man of science go on with perseverance, and let him not take any mischievous delight in flinging his hypotheses at the Word of God. Let the theologian also prosecute his inquiries with diligence and devoutness, and let him give over calling men of science by evil names. They seem often to be working against each other; but they are in reality working for each other and for the truth. In the formation of the tunnel through Mont Cenis, the workmen began at opposite ends, and approached each other with driving machines apparently directed against each other, but met at length in the middle to congratulate each other on the completion of their great undertaking, because they were working under the same supervision. So it will be with our theologians and men of science. God, the great architect of providence, is superintending both; and by and by, through the labors of both, the mountain of difficulty will be tunnelled through, no more to form a barrier in the inquirer's way.

You may do much also in this matter by calling attention to such principles as these, namely: that the Bible was not designed to be a revelation of physical science; that its references to all such subjects are merely incidental, and made in popular language; that, if it had alluded to such subjects in other than popular language, it would have been unintelligible to those to whom it was first given, and would have been rejected by them for containing that which some modern philosophers complain that it does not contain; that, considering the fact that it refers only incidentally to these topics, its language concerning some of them is occasionally very striking, and fully in harmony with modern discoveries; and finally, that considering the course of things in the past, and how what seemed at one time to be in hopeless antagonism to God's Word, is now held intelligently and consistently with it, the wise course will be for both sides to wait before the one tries to prove that there is contradiction, or the other to enforce a harmony.

Moreover, we should not allow it to be forgotten that, all advances of modern science notwithstanding, there will ever be deep, solemn, all-important experiences in the human soul which only God's Gospel can meet; and if we dig down to these we shall go so much lower than science, that the water which she has apparently drawn from our well will return into our spring. There will still be the poison of sin, which no earthly antidote can neutralize, and which can be counteracted only by the blood of the Redeemer's cross. There will still be the sorrow of bereavement, to be solaced only by the vision of the angel at the door of the sepulchre, and the hearing of his soothing words, "Why seek ye the living among the dead? He is not here; He is risen as He said; come see the place where the Lord lay." There will still be the sense of lonesomeness stealing over the heart, even amid the bustle, and business, and prosperity of the world, to be dispelled only by the consciousness of the Saviour's presence. There will still be the spirit-shudder at the thought of death, which only faith in Christ can change into the desire to depart and to be with Him, which is far better. For these things science has no remedy, and philosophy no solace, and, strong in its adaptation to these irrepressible necessities of the human heart, the Gospel of Christ will outlive all philosophical attack and survive every form of scientific unbelief.

But though all that is true, I would not have you speak of Religion and Science as if they were antagonists. They are elder and younger sister in the same family; and though occasionally they may seem to be at variance, yet let but some deep grief enter into the home, or some heavy calamity fall upon the dwelling, and all misunderstanding between them will disappear; they will lock them-

selves in each other's arms, and science will find
her resting-place on the bosom of religion. You
can afford, therefore, to bid science God-speed!
Her triumphs will in the end contribute to the Gospel's advancement. Is it not written, " All things are
yours "? And you may rest assured that truth in
one department can never falsify that which, on its
own evidence, has been already ascertained to be true
in another.

And now, gentlemen, I have reached the end of my
labors among you ; and while there is a sense of
liberty in my heart, to which for months it has been
a stranger, inasmuch as I have now relieved myself
of that load of responsibility which my acceptance of
this Lectureship put upon me, yet I cannot part from
you, with whom I have been brought even so slightly
into contact, without some emotion. I trust that I
have said nothing that may tend to lower your ideal
of the office of the ministry, or to damp the ardor of
your enthusiasm as you look forward to its holy calling. You have before you the noblest work that is
given man to do upon the earth. You will have
cares, and trials, and sorrows, which sometimes may
be heavier than those of others; but you will have
also joys, that are more thrilling and enduring. I
have seen many varieties of experience among my
fellow-men, and have had many ups and downs in my
own ministry. There are many things which I should
not do again if, with my present knowledge, I were
permitted to begin life once more. But even if that

opportunity were afforded me, I would choose again to be a minister of the Gospel, only with more enthusiasm and self-sacrifice than ever. I desire to say with the sainted Henry Martyn, " Thank God, I am Christ's minister." *Christ's minister.* Let that thought fill your souls, and then your service will be of the best. Be not like the cuckoo, whose ever changeless song is the repetition of its own name. Resemble rather the little sky-lark of my native land, which rises ever, singing as it soars, until, itself unseen, it rains a shower of melody upon the listening earth. Forget yourselves. Seek only and always the good of souls and the glory of the Lord, then added to your own happiness will be the joy of every one whom you have brought to Christ; and in the end "When the chief Shepherd shall appear, ye shall receive a crown of glory that fadeth not away." On that day may I be a witness of your happiness and a sharer of your reward!

PASSAGES OF SCRIPTURE QUOTED OR REFERRED TO.

INDEX.